VINCENZO VENEZIA

how to control your emotions

Practical Handbook for Understanding Your Triggers, Turn Off Negative Spirals and Regain your Balance

Contents

INTRODUCTION

It is a well-known fact that emotions have a profound influence on our lives and our health. If you've ever felt frustrated, anxious, or just plain sad, you know how emotions can affect your day-to-day life. They have the power to give you energy and the feeling that you can take on the world, or they can leave you feeling worn out and depleted.

Some people are naturally happy and upbeat, while others suffer from frequent bouts of depression. Either way, you can't escape negative emotions' influence on your life. Emotions drive our lives—they are like the fuel that keeps us going throughout our busy days and too-long nights. Everyone experiences emotions. Sometimes these feelings are fleeting and mild, while others can last for hours or even days at other times. These intense emotions are what psychologists call "negative." They are most often associated with a gloomy state of mind and are known to affect our physical health. Many people find themselves in a constant battle with negative emotions and anxious feelings.

If left unchecked, these issues can take a serious toll on our well-being and our relationships.

The dangers of unchecked negative emotions are now well known to researchers. The leading cause of illness in the modern world, according to the World Health Organization, is stress. Stress can raise your risk of developing depression and anxiety, in addition to a variety of other mental illnesses. And because negative emotions can accumulate over time, even positive people can be affected by them if they are not managed properly.

It's likely that you're reading this book because you've had some unpleasant feelings in the past. Perhaps you've been feeling stressed lately, or the demands of your busy life are beginning to overwhelm you. You want to learn how to manage these feelings before they take over your life. You can learn to ride the wave of negative emotions rather than letting them run you over if you have the right knowledge and abilities.

Learning about the effects of negative emotions is only half the battle. Our emotions influence our health and well-being, but they do so indirectly. For instance, feeling stressed can cause an increased heart rate and blood pressure as your body prepares to face a perceived threat. On the other hand, feeling happy can decrease your heart rate and lower your blood pressure as a natural response to positive feelings. Hormones and chemicals called neurotransmitters drive these emotional changes in your brain.

When you're faced with negative emotions, your brain releases chemicals that cause physical changes in the body that ultimately result in poor health or illness. If you are sad, your brain floods the body with chemicals that make you want to withdraw from others. If you're happy, your brain releases chemicals that make you want to socialize and engage in healthy behaviors. The key is understanding these changes and learning how to live a happy, healthy life despite the bad feelings that occasionally surface!

The book will provide tools to help you manage your negative emotions, and techniques for dealing with them when they arise. You will learn precisely how to recognize your emotions and when they are controlling your life, and discover what to do to quickly regain control. You will also learn some of the most effective ways of addressing these feelings to direct them toward a more productive and healthy outcome. Finally, you will learn exactly when it is appropriate to act on your negative emotions to make the most positive impact on your own life. The concepts and techniques in this book will make your life easier, happier, and healthier.

This book has been purposely structured in three parts to facilitate the assimilation of concepts. The first part will help you to understand emotions, to identify the different negative emotional states including how they work at the brain level and the adverse effects they generate on our bodies. In the second part, we will address all of the techniques and strategies to manage negative "out-of-control" emotions that cause malaise. On the other hand, the third part will help you understand all the situations in which it is appropriate to let the feelings flow because not everything can be controlled and how do the opposite would be harmful.

PART 1 - WHAT ARE NEGATIVE EMOTIONS?

CHAPTER 1: WHAT ARE EMOTIONS?

I n this first chapter, I will try to list the primary negative emotions. This chapter was made specifically for those who perceive intense and prolonged negative feelings but cannot identify the cause of what triggers them. Anyone in this condition will finally be able to unearth the primary negative emotion of discomfort and subsequently learn how to handle it better. For those who are already aware of the negative emotional state they are in, they can also quickly read this chapter and move on to the next chapter.

The term "emotion" refers to an experience that is consciously felt, especially as an intense mental state centered around a particular object or situation. Emotion is the energy that is transmitted between individuals through the various perceptions of stimuli. Stimuli are anything that triggers a response in an individual. These stimuli are interpreted by the brain and then used to initiate a behavioral reaction. Emotions are frequently accompanied by physical changes like sweating, heart palpitations, or tears, as well as distinct facial expressions involving the eyes and mouth.

The Components of Emotions

Emotions consist of three components:

1. Perception

This is the process that reads and interprets sensory stimuli into emotions. It can be described as entering sensory stimuli through the sensory organs into the brain. This is followed by the transmission of nerve impulses to various parts of the brain, where they are then interpreted as an emotion, similar to how a computer would process and interpret data from a keyboard into an output on a screen. Perception can be influenced by personal experiences, cultural differences, and biological factors.

2. Response

This is the physical and mental reaction that involves the secretion of hormones and chemicals in the body. A response can be either conscious or subconscious, depending on how developed the brain's limbic system is.

A conscious response is the ability to knowingly interpret sensory stimuli like interpreting words on paper. A subconscious response is a physical reaction such as running from danger or freezing from fear. These two types of emotional responses can also be experienced simultaneously.

3. Expression

The final component of an emotion is the ability to communicate and share the experience with other people via facial expressions, body language, and actions. Other people perceive these expressions as a depiction of one's emotion, such as smiling when happy or frowning when angry.

The basic emotions can be broken down into eight categories: joy, sadness, fear, disgust, surprise, anticipation, anger, and trust. However, there are many more that can fit into these larger categories.

Positive Emotions

Positive emotions are usually viewed as more pleasant than negative ones. When an organism feels good about something or is aware that nothing bad will happen, it is generally in a positive emotional state. Positive emotions are usually associated with life-affirming activities, and include feelings of love, joy, pride, and gratitude. However, these emotions are not necessarily limited to major life-changing situations – they can also be experienced during mundane activities like watching a funny film or listening to music.

Negative Emotions

Negative emotional states are characterized by feeling stressed or bad about something that has happened or is happening. They are more complex than positive emotions and involve a more diverse range of emotions. Emotions are usually negative when an organism feels threatened by something or someone that is physically and mentally harmful. Negative emotions include anger, sadness, and grief. These are usually not pleasant feelings to experience and can be associated with feelings of anxiety and depression. They are also associated with lack of sleep and constant stress.

According to the APA Dictionary of Psychology, negative emotions are "an unpleasant, often disruptive, emotional reaction designed to express a negative effect. The pursuit of one's goals cannot be advanced when one is experiencing negative emotion." Negative emotions are generally temporary, but they greatly affect behavior and cognition.

Types of Negative Emotions and Common Triggers

Each of these emotions has a specific purpose and causes varying effects on the body and mind. Some negative emotions include anger, emptiness, frustration, inadequacy, helplessness, fear, guilt, loneliness, depression, overwhelm, resentment, failure, sadness, and jealousy.

Anger

Anger is an emotional response in which one experiences hostility and disapproval toward an individual or a situation. Anger can be passionate or violent, particularly when one gets mad about something important to them. It can also be passive, like when you roll your eyes at something that depresses you. Anger is usually associated with frustration, sadness, and fear.

When someone is angry, they may feel:

- A quickened heart rate

- Hot, flushed skin

- A tightening in the throat or chest

- A clenched jaw or tightness in the stomach

- Feelings of agitation, impulsiveness, and anxiety

- An inability to reason clearly and decide wisely (this is linked to the fight-or-flight response)

Common Triggers

There are many causes of anger, but some of the most frequent ones include:

a. Mistreatment of Unfairness

One of the most frequent causes of anger in people is being treated unfairly. It may be an actual incident of being disrespected, treated unfairly, insulted, or threatened, or they may just perceive these things, even if they are not truly happening. Since anger is used to express disapproval, it is a natural response that many people will experience in this type of situation.

b. Poor Communication

Another reason people experience anger is due to poor communication. It could be a misunderstanding that leads to hurt feelings between two or more people. Perhaps someone said or did something without considering how it would affect the other person(s). Alternatively, it could be that someone did not say anything out of fear of saying the wrong thing and having a big argument. This can lead to feelings of frustration, inadequacy, and anger.

c. Lack of Safety

Another reason for anger is a lack of safety. This can happen in one of two ways:

- Perceived safety issues: When they believe they are being threatened, harassed, or bullied, many people experience a lack of safety.

- Real safety issues: Another type of anger is when there

is true danger within a situation. This can occur both in the physical and emotional domains.

d. Feelings of Inadequacy

Sometimes people get angry because they feel inadequate or immature due to some experience (e.g., they fail at something they tried to do). They come to believe it would have been better if they had never attempted the task and wish they could go back in time.

Since it frequently arises unexpectedly and feels out of the blue, anger is a challenging emotion to manage. Likewise, it can be very difficult to observe or notice how anger affects us and how we react when we feel it.

Anger can be a healthy emotion when it helps you stand up for yourself, others, or an important cause, teaches you something about life, connects you with others in your community, creates change, and makes things just if they were not before. Without anger, there wouldn't be much of a reason to seek out justice and fairness. It is also a critical emotion for human relationships, as it helps strengthen bonds between people by letting others know when you need something from them or when they have not fulfilled their obligations to you. However, anger can be very problematic when it triggers aggressive behavior or keeps people stuck in destructive thinking patterns that hurt themselves and those around them.

Emptiness

Emptiness is the lack of a desire or need for something. Emptiness is usually accompanied by feelings of restlessness, boredom, and discontent, as well as a lack of purpose. Those who experience this emotion may feel hopeless, and even suicidal. Some people cannot deal with the emptiness in their lives, so they try to fill the void with a substance or experience.

When someone is experiencing emptiness, they might experience:

- Restlessness and boredom

- Loss of interest

- Lack of motivation and purpose in life

- Feelings of complete hopelessness

- Suicidal tendencies

- A feeling that they have nothing to live for

- Feeling trapped in some way

- Irritability

- Compulsiveness and inability to say no

- Feelings of anger and contempt toward the person who

caused them to feel this way

Common Triggers

Situations that can lead to feelings of emptiness include:

a. Loss of Possession or Things

Some people can experience emptiness due to the loss of possession or thing that gave them personal satisfaction or fulfilled a need in their life.

Emptiness can also result from losing someone who was once a part of our life. Emptiness is often felt when someone becomes uninterested in something they once pursued, such as a relationship with another person. This can be due to people growing apart and not being interested in what they once had or because something with the other person changed. It can also occur because the relationship was flawed or not the way it once was, or because it was never what the individual really wanted.

b. Lack of Growth

Some people experience emptiness when they feel like their lives lack growth. This can occur when one feels unfulfilled and like life has moved forward without them. Emptiness may result from negative or unhealthy experiences and the inability to further develop in a particular area.

Emptiness can also occur when life does not provide an opportunity for further development or experience. People may feel as though they are stuck in a cycle where they cannot move past a certain point in their lives. They might feel trapped and unable to change directions or try different things.

c. Egocentrism

Sometimes people get empty because of egocentrism. This is a less serious kind of emptiness because it does not feel like something is wrong with the person, and they may not even realize they are experiencing this. They may think that they have always had this empty feeling and there is nothing wrong with them. Sometimes the problem is that the person believes nothing matters, which may indicate other problems.

d. Fulfillment of Desire in Another Area

Sometimes people experience emptiness when their life is fulfilled in another area, such as a relationship or career.

A good example is an individual who works all the time and never has any fun or entertainment. This person may think they can only be happy once they reach a certain career goal or make a certain amount of money. The individual may not understand that they can find fulfillment through other means that do not require money.

e. Lack of Self-Esteem

Some people experience emptiness when they have low self-esteem. People who feel this way often do not trust their own emotions or feelings and are unable to acknowledge what they are going through. They may convince themselves their feelings do not matter and that there is something wrong with them as people.

Emptiness can also happen when people feel lost and like they are missing something, but they cannot figure out what it is.

Emptiness is a very common emotion. It is not just something that occurs in a few people's lives but rather an emotion that can happen to well-adjusted and healthy people. Emptiness is often a good thing because it can make a person want to change their lives for the better, so people should try to understand it and learn how to deal with it.

Frustration

Frustration is a feeling of being unhappy with something or someone and wanting to change it or being unhappy that something has not happened in the way you wanted or has not happened at all. Sometimes this feeling results from having a goal that has not been met, particularly when there is no chance to try again.

When someone is frustrated, they might experience:

- Irritability and moodiness

- Increased heart rate and blood pressure

- Restlessness

- A feeling of being trapped or uncomfortable

- Feeling powerless over what is occurring and not being able to change it

- Avoidance of situations that cause frustration

- Difficulty concentrating and finding the right words

- Trouble thinking clearly and making good decisions

- Inability to solve problems correctly or manage stress well

Common Triggers

Situations that can cause frustration include:

a. Dissatisfaction

Frustration can result when a person does not feel satisfied with how a situation is playing out or how an individual is being treated. These issues are often minor, but sometimes they frustrate people because of how important the issue is to them personally. Some people have these issues because they do not know what to do or what to expect in a particular situation.

b. Lack of Information

Sometimes it is impossible to fix a situation because you do not have all the necessary information. This could be due to a number of things, such as time restrictions or other issues. People can become frustrated when they need more information than they have in order to complete a task, or when they cannot access the information they need and are powerless to do anything about it.

c. Loneliness and Loss

Frustration often results from losing something or being lonely and wanting something but not being able to get it. It may be that the person or people who would give you the desired thing are not available and cannot do so. This is a very common cause of frustration, particularly in children.

d. Pressure

Pressure can also cause frustration and make people feel trapped. People often feel this when trying to do something that they believe will benefit them in some way, but their efforts harm them instead. Situations that may cause pressure for people include:

- Attempting to do too many tasks at once

- Trying to keep up with one's responsibilities

- Trying to cope with things that happen without expressing any feelings

- Trying to hold back emotions

- Trying to live up to other people's expectations

- Trying to do things that you do not want to do

- Trying to be perfect

- Feeling unable to get out of a bad situation you are in

- Feeling overwhelmed by too much stress or pressure from the outside world, such as school, family, media, etc.

- Being told what to do with little room for input from your end

e. Pain

Some people are more sensitive to pain than others. People often feel frustrated or trapped when they are in pain – either physical or mental – and cannot get away from it or through it. It is also frustrating when a person is in pain but cannot communicate that to others or ask for help. It can be difficult for other people to understand the pain or frustration that someone is experiencing, especially if it is not physical.

Frustration can be a healthy or unhealthy, depending on the situation. Often, frustration motivates a person to get things done or to accept that they cannot do something and move on to another important goal.

Sometimes, too, frustration is simply what a person feels when they are tired. Frustration can also be a form of anger or something that reminds them of how they were upset when they were younger. However, frustration makes people less flexible in their thinking and more aggressive toward others, which in turn contributes to negative behavior.

Inadequacy

Inadequacy is the perception that one is not competent or has not been given the capacity to perform a task.

When someone is feeling inadequate, they might feel:

- Like they cannot do something well or well enough

- Like they are not capable of doing something

- Like they are not capable of being successful

- Disappointed in themselves

- Frustrated with how others treat them

- As if they are worthless because they cannot perform a task that others can

- Like no one will want them, or that they are not good enough to do something that other people can do

- Like they chose the wrong career path, were not smart enough or did not work hard enough

- Like their talents are hurting them instead of helping them, and they deserve better

Common Triggers

Some things that can make a person feel inadequate include:

a. Feeling stuck

Inadequacy can result when a person wants something to happen but feels stuck in the situation and cannot do anything about it. They may know of other people who have found success in similar situations, and they know there are remedies to overcome the things that are causing them that feeling. However, many people feel stuck or inadequate when they cannot get out of a bad situation themselves, or cannot perform certain tasks.

b. Feeling immobile

Feeling stuck in a bad situation can make a person feel like they are mired in quicksand or living in a bog. If the feeling persists for too long, the person may eventually give up entirely on hoping to make a better life. Frequently, people feel immobile when there are many decisions to be made that are not taken promptly, or they feel stuck because of abusive situations in their life. They may even feel like they have been cut off from the rest of their life or trapped in a situation they cannot get out of on their own.

c. Losing hope

This feeling often comes from the loss of a loved one or someone they have cared for or done things for. Feelings of inadequacy that stem from loss may cause people to lose their appetite and want to eat less because their life seems uncoupled from their health. Many individuals do not consider how unhealthy a situation can feel until a crisis occurs, which forces them to view their situation as hopeless and difficult to overcome.

d. Unsuccessful attempts

People often feel inadequate after they may have tried many things to change their situation, but are unable to do so. This may occur, for example, if someone wanted to move out of their parents' home but was not able to make enough money to do so.

e. Boredom

People can feel inadequate if they are bored with everything. They might not appear interested in anything that has the potential to make them happy, including being around other people. They may feel as though they are merely a shell of who they once were.

Inadequacy is common and can make it hard for some people to cope with the situations they find themselves in. If a person feels inadequate, they may not be able to cope, and yet they are unable to do anything about it because they think they are "stuck."

Inadequacy causes many problems because people often have to deal with their inabilities or the things that keep them from being good enough. Often a person will have learned negative beliefs regarding their own abilities and perceived inabilities, and these beliefs can take a long time to change.

Helplessness

Helplessness can be defined as an inability to change the circumstances of one's situation. When someone feels helpless, they feel as though they cannot take effective action to alter the surrounding environment. Typically, people who feel helpless do not believe in their strength and capabilities and often believe others have complete control.

When someone experiences a sense of helplessness, they may feel:

- Disheartened and sad

- Numb or detached from others and the world around them

- Angry, bitter, or resentful

- Self-doubt, loss of confidence, or a sense of inadequacy in the face of challenges

- Fatigue, low energy levels, lack of motivation

- Depressed or anxious

- As though they are lacking a purpose or place in the world

- Loss of interest in the things they usually enjoy

- Hopeless about their situation

- Grief and despair

- Trapped and as though there is no way out (also known as learned helplessness)

Common Triggers

Some of the situations that can produce feelings of helplessness are:

a. Doing something that you don't have an interest in

Helplessness can be caused when a person is forced to do something they have little or no interest in. They may not have the energy or willpower to do what they want to do, making them feel hopeless about themselves and their actions. This can cause a person to feel like they have no power over the situation, which can affect their daily life and everyday tasks.

b. Feeling like you lack the skills and abilities to improve your situation

A sense of helplessness can also arise when a person does not believe there is anything they can do to deal with their situation. They may feel like this is just how other people treat them, or that this is just what everyone else feels when they fail at something or cannot make it work out as they want. This can also result from being raised by a parent who continually told them they were not good enough. Some people have come to believe all the negative things they hear others tell them, and as a result, they feel helpless towards every new situation or opportunity that arises.

c. Unrealistic expectations

When people have unrealistic expectations of themselves or others, they can feel let down when they cannot do what they desire. A person may place huge expectations of themselves without considering the many situations or barriers that could hinder them from doing the things they want. A person may also have unrealistic expectations of others, which can lead to similar disappointments.

d. Being dependent on others for assistance or support

Because they may believe they have no control over their lives, people who depend on others for their necessities may experience feelings of helplessness. People may get into situations where they cannot take care of themselves and need others to help them manage their life.

e. Difficulty dealing with people or conflict

When a person is unable to deal with people or conflict, it can cause feelings of helplessness. If someone does not know how to get along with other people or handle a situation, they may come to believe there is nothing that can be done about it. They might feel trapped and without options, because they believe there is nothing that can be done to stop the situation from happening.

A sense of helplessness is an automatic response to the perception of being trapped. The belief that a situation is not susceptible to change or that one's actions will not affect the outcome of a situation can elicit feelings of helplessness. People experience this emotion when they feel they have no control and believe their actions are futile in changing the situation. It is thought that helplessness results from a pessimistic view of the world, which causes the affected individual to underestimate their capabilities.

Feelings of helplessness can also be maladaptive. When someone feels trapped in a situation where they believe they ought to have control, they may become overwhelmed with negative emotions that are difficult to deal with. This causes the person to focus on the problem rather than other things happening around them.

Fear

Fear is the overpowering physical reaction that occurs in an organism when it expects danger or a grave threat. It is commonly expressed as an intense feeling of tension and apprehension. This usually occurs when something is present that threatens an individual's well-being, such as loud noises, a sudden appearance, or a physical attack.

The human body usually experiences these feelings through:

- Shivering, sweating, blushing

- Increased heart rate

- Increased breathing (hyperventilation)

- Sweating palms and hands

- Tightness in the chest

- Difficulty breathing or swallowing

- Difficulty seeing anything clearly and generally feeling vague (blurred vision)

Common Triggers

Some situations that can trigger fear include:

a. Lack of trust

A person can feel afraid when they do not trust someone or something. They may be scared that others will leave them without reason or somehow harm them. This feeling can make people unsure what to do in a situation and unsure if they can survive whatever is happening. Fear can also make it difficult to devise a plan in tough situations.

b. Unfamiliarity

Feeling unfamiliar with a situation can cause fear because people do not understand what is happening and what to do. They may find it challenging to create a plan as a result because they are unsure of the necessary actions or choices. People who feel helpless in their lives might also feel bad about themselves and want to exert control over their surroundings to get rid of unpleasant situations or feelings. This can also make it hard for them to focus on the actions they need to take.

c. Observing others

Observers can feel fear when watching someone do something dangerous or scary, such as witnessing a car wreck, fire or even a violent scene from a movie. The inability of the observer to help the person when they are in these situations can make them feel bad about themselves for not being able to help them in their hour of need and for helplessly watching things get worse. This can also make them feel they have no control over the situation.

d. Intense mental or emotional trauma

People may feel afraid during a traumatic event, such as a physical or verbal assault or an experience that leaves them in shock or confusion. This fear can also continue into the aftermath of the trauma. This feeling can be hard to cope with because it makes people unsure of how to handle situations around them, causing them to either be afraid of everything or to avoid anything that may remind them of the event that caused their feelings and emotions in the first place.

e. Lack of personal power

Feeling powerless can instill fear because a person may feel as though they do not have any control over their own lives. It can also make people feel as if everything that is happening to them or around them is beyond their control.

Fear is a response to a perceived threat in the present, and a state of being that can cause one to feel vulnerable, weak, and powerless. Fear involves the fight-or-flight response, where humans either confront the threat or retreat. Fear may be appropriate when great harm is anticipated, but often it serves little purpose. In extreme cases, fear can immobilize people, making them unable to flee or defend themselves. Sometimes fear can persist long after the danger has passed, limited attention is diverted from the feared scenario, and precautions against feared outcomes are taken in a manner that can cause greater harm than good. Knowing your triggers can help you develop more effective coping skills to manage your fear.

Guilt

Guilt is a very strong feeling of remorse. Feelings of guilt are usually accompanied by negative emotions like sadness or anger, and it can even cause these feelings to increase. Guilt can be related to a lack of control when there is no way to alleviate the situation, or it can be as simple as being unable to repay favors or obligations from others.

When someone feels guilty, they may experience:

- A sense of heaviness in the heart

- Increased anxiety and tension in the body and mind

- A loss of motivation

- Shame, embarrassment, and self-loathing

- Feelings of worthlessness and sadness

- A lack of faith or trust in others

- Feelings of remorse or regret

- Feelings of self-blame and helplessness

Common Triggers

Some situations that can cause guilt include:

a. Not doing what you should have

Not performing a certain task that they ought to have done can make people feel guilty. It can cause them to feel bad because they should have been doing their job, and may have put other people out through their lack of action.

b. Letting people down

Letting people down can make a person feel guilty. This feeling can cause one to feel as though they do not deserve to have others to depend on them. As a result, they might avoid getting close to others so that they do not make the same mistake again, or else they can try their hardest to please the other person so that they do not feel guilty anymore.

c. Regret for previous actions

Hating what you did or things that happened to you can also make a person feel guilty. It may lead to a person overworking themselves in an attempt to make up for their mistakes and get themselves out of their current situation.

When a person feels guilty about doing something wrong, they may put on an act to cover their feelings, or try their best to do everything right in order to atone for their mistakes.

Loneliness

Loneliness is an emotional state which is usually associated with feeling unwanted. The act of being alone can cause people to feel this emotion. Loneliness can lead to negative emotions like anger, depression, frustration, and guilt. These negative emotions often mask the original feeling of loneliness.

When someone is lonely, they may feel:

- Sadness or grief

- Sense of insecurity or inferiority in the presence of others

- Uncertainty

- Feelings of rejection and isolation from society

- Anxiety, dejection, and distress (these emotions often develop from feeling unwanted)

- Resentment and disappointment toward others

- An urge to belong or fit in with others

Common Triggers

Some situations that can cause people to feel lonely include:

a. Being isolated from other people

Being alone can make a person feel sad, and can cause them to forget what it is like to have someone around. If the person is alone by choice, they may feel upset that no one wants to be friends or spend time with them, making them feel unwanted and unloved. People might get upset and angry because they feel they are being mistreated and left behind like they do not matter. This feeling can make people have negative thoughts about being around people. People who feel this way might struggle to be themselves around other people. It can also make a person feel sad and like they do not matter.

b. Loss of a loved one

When a person loses a loved one, they may feel like a permanent piece of themselves has been lost. The loneliness that results is often worse for a person if it is someone who died suddenly. This painful experience can make it difficult for a person to move on.

c. Being away from home

Being away from home can make people lonely because they are not with their family and other important people. They might want to go home but do not know how to explain or fix this situation.

d. Discomfort

Feelings of discomfort can make people feel lonely. There are various forms of discomfort, including feelings like embarrassment, unease, or simply not wanting to be around people when it is not necessary. These feeling can make a person feel isolated, as though they need to change themselves to be loved by others.

Loneliness can be a serious problem for people affected by it. If a person does not feel like anyone wants them around anymore and no one seems to care what happens to them, it can make them feel like nothing of value is left in their life. Loneliness is also a serious concern for people because it can cause a wide range of negative thoughts. There is not much a person can do to get rid of this feeling, but there are things they can do to alleviate the discomfort and make things easier for themselves.

Depression

Depression is a very serious problem that comes from feeling sad and upset for a long time. Depression happens when a person's feelings interfere with their ability to function in their daily routines, and it can be considered a sign of clinical mental illness. Depression causes people to feel empty about the things that used to make them happy, sad, or excited. People suffering from depression may feel like they are the only ones who care about what happens in their lives. There is no point in enjoying themselves anymore because they believe they do not have any-one who wants them around.

When someone is depressed, they may experience:

- Changes in appetite and sleep patterns

- A decrease or loss of energy or motivation

- Low self-esteem and a lack of interest in activities

- Irritability and restlessness

- Weight gain or loss, difficulty concentrating, fatigue, chronic pain, headaches

- Suicidal ideation (thinking about suicide) and anxiety

- Inability to think clearly or make decisions

- Constant sadness, worry, and fear

- Inability to enjoy anything like they used to

- Overwhelming feelings of hopelessness, worthlessness, and self-loathing

Common Triggers

Some common triggers for depression include:

a. Life change – the death of a loved one, divorce, physical disability or illness

Depression can be caused by the despair of being unable to do what one wants because life has become so difficult. A person may feel like they cannot handle the issues that have come up. They may feel empty inside because they cannot do what they want with their lives. In this situation, a person feels hopeless and worthless, and that there is nothing that makes them happy or excited anymore.

b. A family history of depression or mental illness

A person may be prone to depression if it runs in their family, particularly if one or both of their parents have been diagnosed with this condition.

c. Trauma – physical or sexual abuse, assault, natural disaster

A person already prone to mental illness may become depressed if they experience physical or sexual abuse, assault, natural disaster, or other trauma. The two worst things that can happen to a person are when someone dies from something like a car crash or an accident and when someone hurts them so much that they have to leave the situation for their safety. A person already prone to mental illness may become depressed after these events because they feel like they cannot handle the things happening to them.

d. Substance abuse – alcohol or drug use

A person already prone to mental illness may become depressed if they have a history of substance abuse. Due to their inability to manage the emotions induced by drug or alcohol use, they may have a greater propensity to develop an addiction. The person will then become more isolated and prone to depressive episodes.

e. Being poor or unemployed, with no opportunity for advancement

A person prone to mental illness may become depressed if they are constantly struggling to get by. A lack of opportunities for advancement in their lives can cause depression, particularly as it can make a person feel unlovable and purposeless. They may even want to end their own life out of desperation.

Depression is a serious matter that can destroy one's life. It is something that everyone should be aware of, and it is something that many people do not know what to do about. This negative feeling can consume a person and cause them to sit around thinking terrible things about themselves and other people. Because the individual believes no one cares about them, they may feel compelled to harm themselves or others. This can happen if the person is left alone to deal with how they are feeling. Depression can become very serious, but there are steps that one can take to stop it from ruining their life.

Overwhelm

Overwhelm can often lead to depression, sadness, and stress. It results from feeling as though there are too many things and people in a person's life. When overwhelmed, one feels as though they have too many responsibilities and tasks to complete. The difference between helplessness and overwhelm is that helplessness is a feeling a person has when they cannot change their situation. Overwhelm results when a person feels they cannot cope with their responsibilities.

When experiencing overwhelmed, one may feel:

- A loss of composure and physical functioning

- Confusion as to what to do next

- A sense of loneliness (i.e., not feeling understood by others)

- Anxiety or panic

- A sudden loss of hearing (which may be associated with hyperacusis)

- Trapped

- Physical and mental inertia or "brain fog"

- Irritation, frustration, annoyance

- As though nothing they do is good enough

- Preoccupation with a variety of subjects at the same time ("multitasking")

- Triggering of any panic attacks (particularly if the overwhelmed person has a pre-existing panic disorder)

Common Triggers

Some of the most common triggers that can cause someone to feel overwhelmed are:

a. Overly busy schedules

Overly busy schedules can trigger feelings of overwhelm. This is especially true for individuals who dislike being alone but also fear being surrounded by others.

Intense feelings, thoughts, and memories about death, dying, or suicide can also cause overwhelm. The person may feel like the world is ending or that there is no one else in the world who cares about them. It is not uncommon for those with social phobia, social anxiety disorder, and other disorders to feel overwhelmed by all the activities they have to keep up with.

Some people may feel overwhelmed by the dangers or risks of quitting drugs/alcohol or the social consequences (or lack thereof) of ending or "quitting" a substance abuse habit.

A person recovering from addiction may be overwhelmed by fear of relapsing, of being caught out by drug tests, a fear that they will relapse if they stop, and fear of their next day being wasted if they do not meet their substance use obligations.

b. Pressure from another person

Pressure from another person can cause overwhelm. A person may feel like their choices are being made for them. This is particularly common when dealing with someone with a narcissistic personality disorder who has an inflated sense of self-importance.

When someone is under this kind of pressure, they may feel as though they are being controlled and manipulated by the other person, which can cause feelings of helplessness or even self-hatred. People with borderline personality disorders may also feel overwhelmed when their significant others try to make decisions. People in abusive relationships may also experience overwhelming feelings, or that they are not allowed to make choices on their own.

c. Getting into financial trouble

When a person gets into financial trouble, it can cause feelings of overwhelm. Common feelings that people experience when they get into huge amounts of debt are:

- Depression about the mounting debt and increasing interest rates from the loans/credit cards

- Fear that creditors may demand payment of all debts immediately, or fear of being arrested for failing to repay loans, or for not repaying them in time.

- Shame that one is in such a position

- Guilt over not being able to afford the necessities in life

- Regret that one has spent so much money and borrowed so much that they now find themselves in a position they never anticipated.

Many individuals feel overwhelmed by their financial situation. They may feel angry at themselves for spending too much or accumulating so much debt, which can leave them frustrated and drained.

d. Trying to fit in

People trying to make their partners happy, or trying to fit in with a particular social group can get overwhelmed by all the activities that need to be done or the responsibilities being asked of them. This is particularly prevalent when a person does not know how to say "no."

People who do not want to stand out from their friends/acquaintances may feel overwhelmed by making decisions that they think will be more "normal," so they don't stand out from the crowd.

e. Fears about the future

Being overwhelmed by fears about one's future is also very common. Common fears that cause feelings of overwhelm include:

- Fear of not having enough money

- Fear of losing a job or not being able to find another one.

- Fear of being alone (this may be a result in part from an earlier relationship that was unstable, abusive, and dysfunctional)

- Health concerns

Those who worry about what will happen in their future can feel overwhelmed by these worries and be constantly on guard against some disaster that they fear could occur at any time.

Being overwhelmed can lead to low self-esteem, unhappiness and loneliness. It can also cause feelings of stress and tension, isolation, worthlessness, shame, and despair. Overwhelm can cause a person to re-evaluate their lives, beliefs, and values as they enter a state of crisis. Being overwhelmed may also make it hard for a person to see the positive things in their life or the present moment; this is especially true if they have been used to seeing only the negatives for many years. Having a low sense of self-worth and feeling like a failure is also common when a person feels overwhelmed. Although many people who experience overwhelm have some positive aspects of their lives, they may feel overwhelmed by the one negative aspect they are most afraid of, which causes them to lose sight of all the positive aspects.

Resentment

Resentment is a feeling of anger and hostility that occurs when one believes they have been treated unjustly. It can cause people to feel bitter towards others and wish for retribution. Resentment is often a response to an individual's inability to attain an expected outcome or goal they have worked hard to achieve.

When someone is experiencing resentment, they may feel:

- Sad or depressed

- Tired

- Defensive or angry

- Frustrated

- Worn out

- Humiliated or embarrassed

- Insecure and needy for reassurance, approval, or even safety

- Confrontational and defensive

- Alienated

- Anxious or nervous

Common Triggers

People can become resentful over just about anything. However, some common triggers include:

a. Feeling neglected

Those who feel they are being neglected can become resentful when a relationship or friendship turns sour. This is often seen in abused children, who often resent their parents and the person who abused them.

b. Being lied to or cheated on

Many people feel resentful when they believe they have been lied to or cheated on by someone they care about. This can leave them feeling angry or hurt, not just towards the person who was unfaithful to them, but also towards themselves for believing that their partner was the right person for them. Some people can experience long-term resentment and trust issues because of being cheated on and may decide that they would rather be alone than suffer through another relationship or marriage like the one they had before.

c. Being abused

When someone is being abused, it's very easy for them to develop long-term resentment towards their abuser. They may feel angry about what happened and even become depressed for being put in this situation. They may also feel like the abuse is their fault or that they could have done more to prevent it from happening. But those who were abused often believe they can't do anything to stop the abuse from happening again, which leads to feelings of helplessness. All of these feelings can be signs of resentment.

d. Being taken for granted

Being taken for granted is not a common reason for resentment, but it happens occasionally. This often happens between a parent and child but can also happen in a romantic relationship or even in friendships when one person feels like the other is being too demanding or taking advantage of the other without giving anything back in return.

e. Feeling unappreciated

Feeling unappreciated is a common reason for resentment in relationships, friendships, marriages, and any other type of interpersonal relationship. It is easy to take someone or something for granted if they are always present, but resentment grows when they are no longer appreciated and respected. This can also be why couples get divorced; when one partner starts to feel taken advantage of or unappreciated within the relationship, they may resent their partner and then eventually leave them for someone else.

Resentment is a common emotion that many people experience at some point in life. It can lead to unhealthy thoughts and behaviors, such as ruminating and victim-blaming.

Failure

A sense of failure happens when a person cannot achieve a certain goal in life. This is often due to their own physical and mental limitations

When Someone experiences failure, they may feel:

- Ashamed and guilty

- Sad or depressed

- Loss of self-confidence

- Impatience and anxiety

- Self-blaming thoughts

- Resentful and angry

Common Triggers

Common triggers that can lead to a sense of failure include:

a. Being rejected from a goal or place of interest

If they are turned down for something they have been pursuing a while, many people, including teenagers and young adults, may feel like failures. This can cause someone to feel sad and depressed because there was something that they wanted that they were unable to achieve.

When this feeling of rejection continues over an extended period, it may cause them to become anxious because they believe they are unprepared for the future. This can be a bigger issue for someone if they do not have many friends or their family is not supportive.

b. Not living up to parental expectations

If a parent's expectations are very high, then it is likely that their child will often feel like they are a failure because they can never seem to reach those expectations. Some examples of this type of parent include coaches and sports parents who expect their children to win every game no matter what obstacles come in the way. These parents expect their children to be perfect and may put them down if they make any mistakes.

This event can make a person feel guilty for not being good enough or like a failure for not meeting their parent's expectations.

c. Feeling bad about a decision that was made

Sometimes it is beneficial for someone to experience failure so they can learn from their mistakes in the future. However, sometimes people feel like failures when they make even the smallest of mistakes. For example, suppose a person made a decision that resulted in something bad happening to someone else, such as punching someone in school or leaving behind an expensive appliance while moving into a new place. In that case, they may feel like they are not living up to their family expectations or as though they have let down the people who trusted them.

Feeling like one is not living up to one's own or other people's expectations can make someone sad and depressed. This can lead to poor decision-making, poor grades and many other negative ways of dealing with emotions.

d. Failure to live up to a stereotype

People from certain backgrounds or social classes may often experience a sense of failure because they do not fit their group's expectations. For example, a person from a certain socioeconomic background may feel like a failure if they are not successful in their career and personal life. They may start to believe that there is no place for them in society and that they will never be able to achieve any goals or be content with their lives; this can make them feel very anxious and even depressed.

e. Having a low opinion of themselves

Some people are just born with low self-esteem, which is often encouraged by society. Because they believe they are not good enough at anything, this can frequently result in resentment and anger. This can cause them to treat themselves and others negatively, leading to further feelings of sadness, anger, anxiety, and depression. People who have low self-esteem may also make poor choices when it comes to planning their futures or dealing with other issues that come up in life. They may blame their broken lives on external factors rather than learning from their mistakes.

Failure is something that can be learned from. Successful people can often relate to the experience of failure, and failure is more common than success in the life of most people. It should be a lesson taken with a grain of salt and remembered for the future so an individual can learn from their mistakes and avoid making them again. Those who fail will find themselves facing problems they need to solve in order to move on with their lives, but overcoming this is an essential part of life that should result in growth.

Sadness

Sadness is an emotion that occurs when a person experiences a mental state of emotional pain. A person can experience sadness if they hear bad news, if they experience grief or loss, or feel like something bad is going to happen. Sadness can cause someone to feel negative emotions such as hopelessness toward their problems, thoughts of suicide, and even feelings of anger.

When someone is sad, they may experience:

- Annoyance or irritation

- Excessive fatigue, exhaustion, and lethargy

- Tearfulness, crying and even sobbing

- Feelings of worthlessness

- Inability to feel pleasure in things they previously enjoyed

- The belief that their life is meaningless

- Inability to concentrate

- Extreme guilt, worry, not feeling deserving of others' love or trust

Common Triggers

Some of the common triggers of sadness are:

a. Unfulfilled or unmet needs

If a person feels like something is missing in their life, it may cause them to feel sad. For example, if a person has an unfulfilled need for love, this can sometimes cause them to feel sad and alone. This can also happen if a person has unfulfilled physical needs such as food, water, and/or shelter.

Sadness caused by unmet needs can also arise if someone feels like something is missing from their life because of financial, social, or legal barriers. This can cause someone to feel that their life is meaningless, which can lead to feel a sense of hopelessness.

b. Having something to prove

Sadness may occur if a person feels they have something to prove. If a person feels like they need to be successful at everything that they do, they may feel sad if they cannot achieve their goal. For example, suppose someone works hard at their job but is not getting promoted and is being passed up for raises. This can cause feelings of sadness and anger because they feel like they are not good enough or are not getting recognition for all their work.

c. Lack of self-confidence or self-esteem

When a person does not have the confidence or self-esteem that they deserve, they feel sad. Some people may experience low self-esteem when their appearance, weight, and other things about themselves are not good enough according to the standards of society and their parents.

A person may also experience sadness and depression if they don't think they are good enough to be around other people. It may also lead them to start feeling as though they do not deserve the things they want or that they do not deserve the love of others. Sometimes people who experience low self-esteem will even start acting recklessly or putting themselves into dangerous situations because they feel it is better than being alone or unhappy. They may also become extremely withdrawn.

d. Feelings of worthlessness

Feelings of worthlessness can lead to sadness. This may occur if a person believes they are not deserving of things such as love, money, attention, etc. People who do not feel they deserve good things such as love and attention may put themselves in dangerous situations where their lives can be endangered.

e. Attempts at self-destruction

Sadness can occur when people want to hurt or kill themselves. Some people who experience mood disorders such as depression or bipolar disorder will put themselves into dangerous situations when experiencing extreme sadness and anger.

Everyone is different, so these issues may not necessarily cause sadness in everyone but can often be the reason someone feels this way. Sadness can lead to depression, withdrawal, and pessimism. Long-lasting feelings of sadness can cause people to have a pessimistic outlook on life and can lead to them being unable to concentrate on anything but the cause of their sadness. They may begin to feel that nothing they do has meaning and that they are not worth the love and effort from others.

Sadness can affect people mentally, physically, and emotionally.

Jealousy

Jealousy is an emotional response to something threatening an individual's relationship with another, like a partner or friend. Jealousy can be either reactive or proactive. Reactive jealousy involves feeling upset about a partner being unfaithful and wanting to compete for their attention. Proactive jealousy involves thinking about ways to become more attractive and earn more affection from friends and family members.

When someone is jealous, they may feel:

- Worried and insecure

- Distrustful of others

- Close-minded

- Resentful and bitter towards their partner or loved ones (this is why jealousy is such a big cause of conflict in relationships)

- Angry, hateful, and vengeful

- Anxious about the possibility of a threat to one's relationship with a loved or family member

- Afraid of losing someone you deeply care about

- Sad, depressed and hopeless

- Misunderstood and alone

Common Triggers

Some of the most common triggers of jealousy are:

a. Insecurity

When a person is feeling insecure, they are more likely to feel jealous. Because they do not believe that others value them as highly as they do other people, people with low self-esteem are less likely to feel secure in their relationships. This can cause people to feel they are easily replaceable and that others will not want to stay with them because they are "not good enough" or "lacking."

b. Feeling left out

When a person is feeling left out, they are more likely to feel jealous. This might be a result of their perception of unfair treatment or their fear of being rejected.. When someone is worried that they will be rejected, they may become overly competitive with others and monitor them too closely to ensure that no one is talking about them behind their backs. This can cause them to feel extremely insecure and jealous of others, particularly those who have more friends than they do.

c. Trust issues

When a person has trust issues, they are more likely to feel jealous. This may be because they were betrayed by someone they once trusted in the past. To regain the trust they feel they have lost, they may become overly competitive with others and try to outperform their loved ones.

d. Fear of loss

When a person is fearful that they will lose something or someone, they can become jealous.

This can make people feel anxious and insecure, which can cause them to act in ways that are not necessarily productive or constructive.

Jealousy can lead to many other negative emotions such as anger, sadness, and depression. One way that jealousy can lead to a negative mental state is by causing worry and anxiety, which can cause a negative outlook on life. Jealousy can also lead to people acting recklessly or aggressively towards others. In addition, jealousy can make people feel paranoid about possible threats against them, which causes them to become extremely withdrawn. Jealousy may even lead people into dangerous situations such as self-harm or suicide because they fear that their parent/friend/spouse does not love them or does not care about their feelings.

Negative emotions are a part of everyday life and are a normal response to the situations we face. The most important thing when it comes to dealing with negative emotions is being able to identify the specific emotion that you are feeling and being able to realize what exactly caused it. Once a person can pinpoint exactly why they are feeling a particular way, they can take the necessary steps to either avoid that situation or learn how to cope with it in a healthy way.

It is important to realize that these negative emotions are only temporary feelings and will soon subside with time if dealt with correctly. When faced with these situations, it is most important to not judge yourself harshly for feeling the negative emotion. This can lead to more emotional issues and make them harder to handle in the future.

Emotions are necessary and, in themselves, are not negative. Therefore, the emotions themselves are not good or bad; they are necessary to help you function and thrive.

CHAPTER 2: NEGATIVE EMOTIONS & THE BRAIN

The human brain is composed of many different parts that work together to control the body. It is very complex and has been studied for hundreds of years, with many scientists trying to understand it better. The brain is responsible for all the emotions you have and the way those emotions control your body. That tiny part of the brain called the amygdala controls our emotions. It sends signals which activate different areas in your brain that trigger emotions (which are then sent back to the amygdala). These signals go through a complex network where they pass back and forth between two areas in particular: the hippocampus and the striatum. These are the areas that are associated with learning. The hippocampus is responsible for long-term memory, and the striatum is responsible for decision-making and reward. When the signals from these two areas reach the amygdala, it causes a "fight-or-flight" reaction, which causes your body to react in a specific way.

These reactions can cause you to feel good when they trigger positive emotions such as happiness, pride, excitement, and love to name a few because when you relive good memories, you feel happy. However, these same reactions can make you feel bad when your amygdala activates another part of your brain that causes anxiety. Suppose you consistently feel anxious when you think about something. In that case, your hippocampus and striatum will try to increase their connections with other parts of your brain to eliminate that anxiety and make a new connection. For example, if you are always thinking about a certain person, they will be connected with your amygdala, which will cause you to feel anxious. When that happens, the hippocampus and striatum will try to find a new network to relieve your anxiety. However, for your body to make this change, it must be stabilized.

If you go through this specific process that changes your brain, then the connection between your amygdala and other parts of your brain will be made so that you no longer feel anxious in certain situations. This new way of thinking will give you more control over how you react to things, which leads to more positive emotions.

Negative emotions can make us feel bad because it does not take much for your body to start creating negative thoughts. Your body only needs a little bit of stimulation to create a new memory or thought. An example of this is something that most people are familiar with: the movie *E.T.* When you watch the movie, the image of an eye staring at you causes your amygdala to activate. This causes your brain to think, "That creature is watching me, and I need to run," which is a negative thought. If such a thing happens enough times, your brain will create negative thoughts and feelings. This is how phobias can develop. However, if you go through the process of changing your brain so you can control your negative thoughts and emotions, then your brain will learn to stop creating them as easily.

The human brain only needs a little stimulation to create memories or thoughts that cause an emotional reaction. Once those memories have been created and connected with our reactions in life, they become part of our identity and can influence our actions without us knowing. The memories of the bad events in life can build up and affect you emotionally, which can then cause anxiety, depression, and sometimes even a lack of motivation.

However, if you learn how the brain creates emotions and how to manage them, you will have more control over your brain. You can remove negative emotions and create positive ones that cause happiness. It may take time to see results, but it is a worthwhile process to go through in order to live a happy life.

The History of the Study of Emotion

Charles Darwin introduced the concept of emotion in 1872 with *The Expression of Emotions in Man and Animals.* This ushered in the first age of emotional studies, known as the Golden Years, to some psychologists. Although this age was short lived, it is considered a defining moment in the history of emotional studies.

Darwin's book inspired the "basic emotion" approach to the psychology of emotion. This approach was popular in the late 20th century, which theorized that different basic emotions could be grouped into categories. This approach saw the study of emotions as subjective feeling states, distinct from physiological responses. This basic emotion view defines emotions according to primary effects such as happiness, sadness, and anger, and it locates the origins of these emotions in specific brain regions. The basic emotion view also sees each emotion as corresponding to a pattern of physiological changes and motivated action tendencies which are conscious rather than innate.

Meanwhile, *What is an Emotion?* by William James, written in 1884, introduced the idea that bodily function produces emotion, not the other way around.

James' theory, which came to be known as the James–Lange Theory, theorized that bodily reaction is a precursor to emotion. The theory states that when we perceive an event as threatening or important, there are changes in our autonomic nervous system (ANS). The ANS controls functions, including the heart rate and blood pressure. These alterations result in cognitive modification and emotional response.

The James–Lange theory also suggests that different emotions often occur together. For example, situations involving threats and feelings of danger often cause us to experience fear, while situations involving rewards and positive experiences give us positive emotions. This is called the Hedonic-Echoic Theory, which states that there are two stages to emotion: hedonic experiences, which are the response to rewards, and echoes which are the response to punishment.

The James–Lange theory has undergone many modifications since its inception in 1884. A major modification was made in the 1920s when John B. Watson published *Psychology from the Behavioral Viewpoint*. This book introduced a behaviorist approach to psychology. The behavioral approach focuses on the observable behavior of animals and analyzes it to determine what happens in the brain to cause that behavior. In this version of the James–Lange theory, emotions are not seen as physiological changes leading up to a cognitive response. Instead, primary emotions are believed to be caused by changes in our body, while secondary emotions are believed to be caused by cognition and thought.

The behavioral view also sees emotionality as learned facts rather than innate attributes of people. People learn an emotional vocabulary and language, which is then used to discuss emotion. This view suggests that emotion is a learned behavior.

This theory, also known as the U-M Theory or The Cattell–MGH Theory of Emotion, argues that emotions are caused by the brain's activity in three principal areas: the standard central network (SVM), the evaluative network (ENV), and core affect system (CAS). The SVM is responsible for sensory stimuli such as sights and sounds. The ENV includes information about how these stimuli affect us emotionally. Finally, the CAS includes cognitive information about these sensory stimuli, processed in higher brain areas such as working memory.

The Cattell–MGH theory broadly parallels the standard view of emotions but adds two more parts. The first is a perceptual system that controls the brain's sensory areas. The second is an action system which serves as a maintainer of our current emotional state. The three systems are interconnected in that sensory inputs can alter your emotions, and actions you take can change your emotional state in response to those stimuli. This view also sees emotionality as learned fact rather than innate attributes of people.

In this theory, the amygdala is the main location for emotion because it is where memories are encoded and stored. This theory suggests that when your brain is learning to encode a memory, you react emotionally to the information being learned.

In 1927, James was countered by Cannon, who theorized that visceral changes are too slow and too ambiguous to cause emotion. He theorized that visceral changes occur in both emotional and non-emotional states. Cannon claimed that the visceral and non-visceral reactions should be treated as two separate dimensions for emotional reactions.

The Cannon-Gauquelin Theory was a modification of James' theory. There are three types of emotional reactions which are visceral (physical/gustatory and kinesthetic), emotional (affective), and somatic. This theory also hypothesizes three emotional areas in the brain stem: the dorsal vagal complex, the ventral vagal complex, and a third area that sits between the two, the dorsal motor complex. The three areas are responsible for visceral, emotional, and somatic responses to stimuli such as food tasting good or bad.

While James' theory inspired Cannon-Gauquelin, the two theories are different in some ways. James recognized that visceral reactions to stimuli such as food tasting good or bad could be emotional reactions, non-physical visceral reactions, or both. Cannon-Gauquelin suggests that only visceral responses are physical and emotional. Likewise, Cannon-Gauquelin does not include emotions caused by cognitive stimuli such as thinking about something good or bad, and this is where it differs from James' theory.

Meanwhile, the Cannon-Bard Theory states that there are two responses to stimuli: physical and emotional. This theory suggests that changes in the ANS are not responsible for changes in emotion but are both a product of emotion and an antecedent to emotion. The Cannon-Bard theory also suggests that cognitive appraisal helps determine our response to a stimulus, and emotions stem from this appraisal process.

Following this turn in emotional studies, behaviorism gained popularity and threw emotional studies into the dark ages for roughly four decades. With the advent of understanding brain function, researchers began to look at different areas of the brain and how they affect emotions. This is where cognitive neuroscience began.

In the 1960s, the study of emotion experienced a renaissance with the introduction of Magda Arnold's *Emotion and Personality*, which introduced the Appraisal Model of emotion. Sylvan Tomkins followed with *Affect, Imagery, and Consciousness* in 1962 and introduced the modern articulation of the current view of emotion. This theory argues that we analyze our emotions through automatic responses like crying, sweating, and smiling. These emotional reactions are then expressed via conscious reactions like facial expressions and body language.

The appraisal model states that emotions are a result of cognitive appraisals. The brain takes information in our environment, analyzes it to determine what is good or bad, and determines our emotional response. If you see something good, you should feel happy, while if you see something bad, you should feel angry. This theory was further developed by Deci in 1965, who argued that we only appraise the worthiness of a stimulus before we respond emotionally to it; he called these appraisals consequential events.

The appraisal model argues that inner responses are the best way to express your emotions. This theory states that it is important for you to feel your emotions in order to use them as guides in response to stimuli such as food tasting good or bad. The appraisal model of emotion has been the predominant theory since it was introduced in 1962.

As we move past the appraisal model and into the 21st century, our understanding of emotion has become more nuanced. We have begun to understand different emotions and how they are expressed under different conditions.

The study of emotion started as obscure and was shunned by the psychological community, but it has since enjoyed a renaissance. The field of psychology has come to understand emotion as an important part of our lives and engaged in research on emotions from the late 19th century to the present.

CHAPTER 3: WHEN ARE NEGATIVE EMOTIONS BAD FOR ME?

Negative emotions can be bad for you if you do not know how to handle them. Negativity can lead to physical and psychological harm, which can be life-threatening if not addressed properly.

Signs of Holding in Negative Emotions

There are numerous potential signs you may be burying or holding in negative emotion. Those include:

Back pain

If you are holding in negative emotions, you may experience back pain. The pain is your body trying to remind you that this emotion is still in you and needs to be released. When you suppress your emotions, this tension can build up over time. This is because your body expends a great deal of additional energy to push negative emotions inward. If the back is not relieved of this tension, it can result in back pain and damage.

Constipation or diarrhea

Your emotions can also affect your digestive system, causing constipation or diarrhea. Holding onto a negative emotion for a long period can cause the body to feel very stressed and anxious. This, in turn, affects the digestive system, making it harder for your body to process food and convert food into energy. When you are not eating regularly, constipation or diarrhea can occur due to stomach acid being unable to break down food easily. This can cause uncomfortable pressure in your abdomen and your large intestine.

Change in appetite

Negative emotions can also change your appetite. This is a very serious sign that your emotions are still being held in and must be dealt with. A change in appetite can signify holding in many negative emotions, which can cause serious health issues if not addressed.

Chest pain

Emotions can also cause chest pain. This could be due to trying to release many negative emotions at once. These pains can be quite frightening, especially if they occur suddenly.

Dry mouth

You may find your mouth very dry if you are holding in many negative emotions. The mouth plays a significant role in regulating stress and releasing negative emotions. The mouth has many muscles controlling it, and those muscles can be used to hold emotions. Therefore, holding on to strong negative emotions may cause your mouth to become very dry.

Extreme tiredness

When your body is on high alert and searching for a way to store the negative emotion, it must use energy in order to do so. As a result, you may experience extreme tiredness, especially in a social situations.

General aches and pains

Negative emotions can also cause serious aches and pains throughout your body. The body uses so much energy that it also causes you to be tense and in pain all over your body. This is a sign of your body and mind going into extreme stress. Thus, when you are holding on to negative emotions, you may feel like many parts of your body are in pain because it is a very stressful activity for your body and mind to work against one another.

Headaches

Trapped emotions can cause headaches. You block your body's energy flow when you hold in negative emotions. Headaches can be caused by holding in negative emotions because this block prevents the proper flow of energy throughout your body. If you continue to hold your emotion in, the headache will become more intense. Though headaches might not seem too big of a deal, they can be very painful and distracting.

Insomnia

We've all heard that stress can cause insomnia, but repressing emotions can also lead to difficulty sleeping. If your body is trying to work through the emotion, it may be unable to rest. This is a very serious indicator of what is occurring in your mind and body and must be addressed immediately (as stress can do even more damage if it continues).

Lightheadedness

When you are holding on to negative emotions, your body has to use a lot of energy to prevent them from coming out. This can cause your body's oxygen supply to drop, which can make you feel faint.

Heart Palpitations

When you feel very emotional, your body will feel like it needs to release the energy it is holding. This means you may feel an irregular heartbeat. If you are holding in negative emotion and not working through it, your body is likely asking itself, "Should I let this emotion out or keep it inside?" While this question is being asked internally, the physical symptom of your heart beating faster can help you identify and move past the emotion.

Sexual problems

When holding on to an emotion, you may have sexual problems. Many people notice that when they are feeling extremely angry at someone or when they are dealing with a lot of stress, their sex drive goes down. This is due to the fact that your body and mind are focused on processing the emotion. Holding on to negative emotions can prevent you from giving your full attention to the sexual experience.

People experiencing sexual problems often do not understand what is happening because they think it is an issue with their relationship or that they are not attracted to their partner. But emotions have a direct effect on the body, and holding in negative ones can mean that your body is not feeling "safe" in the bedroom.

Shortness of breath

When emotions are repressed, your body goes into fight-or-flight mode. When this happens, your breathing often quickens, and you may not feel like you have enough air.

If the body has difficulty releasing negative emotions, you may find yourself taking short, rapid breaths when doing simple tasks, such as walking or talking. This can consume a lot of energy because your body is simultaneously trying to repress your negative emotions while also holding onto them.

Stiff neck

When you repress a feeling or do not permit yourself to feel it fully, your neck can become stiff. As a result, you may have difficulty performing your day-to-day tasks.

Sweating

Sweating is a normal physical reaction, however, on numerous occasions, individuals have suppressed their emotions for so long that they begin to perspire more heavily than usual. This is because their bodies are using energy, trying to keep everything under control and hold back what they are feeling. It may feel like your body is trying to keep you cool, but it is trying to return to normal.

Upset stomach

When emotions are difficult to express, the body may react through a change in the gut. The stomach is one of the organs that can store negative emotions, and when an emotion is too strong or not released, your body will amp up its physical activity to try to get rid of it. This means that you may feel upset in your stomach if you hold on to many negative emotions or have been suppressing them for some time. Your stomach may sometimes feel upset or "hot." This is caused by the body trying to eliminate the negative emotion. The more this happens, the more often your stomach feels uncomfortable. It makes you nauseous and gives you a general feeling of discomfort.

Weight gain or loss

Negative emotions can result in weight gain or loss, especially if the emotion has been held for long periods at a high intensity or level. Negative emotions can lead to comfort eating – and the more you eat to deal with your emotions and stresses, the more weight you gain.

Weight loss can happen similarly, but it is often related to increased toxic feelings. When emotions are repressed, they may be less visible on the outside, but they are still there, and internalizing them can give you the sense that you need to release weight. When your body cannot "bust out" of something or when it feels like something is toxic or blocking access to something, it may try to lose weight as a result. This process can continue for a long time if you are not mindful of what is happening, and can cause serious health issues later on down the line.

It is important to learn how to manage these signs and symptoms if you are experiencing any of them. Consider getting help from a professional therapist that is trained in working through emotions. It can often take longer than you think to learn how to manage your emotions and overcome them, but it will make a big difference in your life.

PART 2 - HOW CAN I CONTROL NEGATIVE EMOTIONS?

CHAPTER 4: IDENTIFYING MY EMOTIONS

Before you can deal with your emotions positively, you need to learn to recognize exactly what it is you are feeling. If you are unable to recognize the emotion you are currently experiencing, it will take much longer for you to become upbeat and less stressed.

Techniques for Identifying Our Emotions

There are several ways in which a person can identify what it is they're feeling, so we are going to look at a few of the most effective ones. Each technique is different in terms of how you can use them and its benefits, so you will want to ensure that you are familiar with them so you can use them safely and correctly.

1. Mindfulness

The first method we'll look at can help you become more aware of your feelings on a regular basis. This is called mindfulness; it allows you to become more aware of what is going on in your life at any given time. This means you will have a better understanding of your emotions, and a greater ability to control them.

a. Mindfulness Meditation

Awareness is an important aspect of meditation; with it, you can identify what negative emotion you are feeling in real-time and better understand its cause. This ensures that you are taking steps to control your emotions in a positive manner. You can use mindfulness meditation on a very basic level, and this is not something that is going to take up a whole lot of time. If you are someone who finds it hard to calm yourself down, this could be the ideal method for you.

How to do it:

Step 1: Sit in a quiet place.

Make sure it is not too light or too dark because you want to keep the mind relaxed. This makes it easier for you to come up with more positive thoughts and identify negative ones. Find somewhere you can remain relaxed for about 15-20 minutes.

Step 2: Close your eyes and relax.

Now that you are in a comfortable place, close your eyes and let your mind wander into a more relaxed state. Pay attention to the body and try to control it a little bit more.

Step 3: Take deep breaths.

Start breathing slowly. Breathe in through your nose and out through your mouth. This will help keep tension at bay and increase the amount of oxygen you are getting into your bloodstream.

Step 4: Pay attention to your thoughts.

You should now focus on the thought in your mind; this is where mindfulness meditation comes in handy. You are much more likely to notice what negative thoughts are going on in when you are in a meditative state rather than just afterward when you've returned to normal consciousness.

You can also ask questions like:

- How long have I been feeling this way?
- Is this a familiar feeling?
- Is this something I have had to deal with before?
- What do I need to fix about myself to feel better?
- Am I worried about something?
- Am I feeling calm or not?
- Do I need to change my thoughts to feel better?

- Am I thinking negatively, and what can I do about it right now?

- What is my mind doing at this moment in time?

Asking questions like these will allow you to get to know yourself better and understand why and how certain feelings are generated. This is where mindfulness shines; it allows you to understand better how you feel daily.

By keeping an eye on your thoughts, you can quickly change the ones that are causing anxiety and stress.

Step 5: Combine breathing with thinking.

Now that you are paying attention to your thoughts, start associating breathing with each thought. This will help keep your mind in check and ensure that you are living in the moment as much as possible.

What does this do?

Breathing deeply helps to calm you down, helping you deal with negative emotions better. This lets you become more aware of what is going on in your mind and helps you make much better decisions on how to handle a certain situations.

The key point of mindfulness is that you are fully aware of what is happening in the moment; this will allow you to keep calm and handle the situations that arise better. It will also help you identify exactly what is causing this reaction so that the next time it happens, you can identify it more easily and deal with it correctly and efficiently.

b. Mindfulness Diary

This method will allow you to monitor your life's events and their emotional effects. If you want to know more about why certain situations make you feel a certain way, then this may help crystallize those feelings. You can also share your mindfulness diary with others in order to help them understand why things happen the way they do; it will be a bit less personal but can be an important tool for those you are trying to help.

What does this do?

This technique helps you understand how your negative emotions are created and make them feel less real. You may also feel a more optimistic outlook on life.

This method permits you to be forthright about what is occurring and why. You will learn how to identify which events cause particular emotions, allowing you to predict what will occur and how it will influence your behavior.

How to do it:

Step 1: Write down your thoughts.

Write down whatever thoughts you would like, but be as precise as possible.

As an example, you can answer the following questions:

Q: What are you doing right now?

A: I am doing ____

Q: What are you thinking about?

A: I am thinking ______________________________________
(you can write how you feel about yourself, the surroundings etc.)

Q: What happened to make you feel this way?

A: ____

Q: What do you think about it?

A: ____

Q: What would you do if you could do anything right now?

A: I would ____

Q: What is worrying you the most at the moment?

A: ____

Q: What do you need in order to feel better?

A: I need ____

Q: How does it feel when you cannot stop thinking about a certain topic?

A: ____
(you can write what the thought is, why it is continuing and what are other ideas might come up if you allow them)

Step 2: Reminder.

After you have answered all of the above questions, you will then create a reminder on a piece of paper or a whiteboard. This reminder will relate to your thoughts so that you never forget them again; put it somewhere you will see it every day so that you are always aware of how you are feeling and what is influencing you.

The reminders could be the following:

a. I can make myself feel better by ____________________
(write down what it will take to make you a better person in the future. This could be anything from getting a new job, becoming more confident, or even changing your outlook on life.)

b.: I want to remember that ____________________

You can write your own reminder, or you can copy someone else's. These reminders can help you remember not to give up, and will help you see the bigger picture when things feel overwhelming. Whatever reaction you had in the past, if you learn to think and react differently in future, all those bad feelings will disappear.

After creating the reminder, you should incorporate it into your daily life. This can be done by posting the reminder on your wall, creating a text reminder, or even just writing it down and carrying it with you. Reminders are great because they give the person something to focus on every single day

This method can help a person involved in self-harm, as it allows them to really think about the cause of their actions and how they want to react to those feelings. Reminders will also help people stop self-harming because they will have a constant reminder in front of them that will ensure that they know there are other options for dealing with the situation.

Step 3: Read the reminder every day.

After you have written your reminder, look at it every single day so you get a better understanding of what is affecting your thoughts. It might be hard at first, but the more often you read it, the less likely it is to bother you. It's possible for people to become so preoccupied with their feelings and thoughts that they stop thinking about other things and eventually lose the ability to focus on anything else. If this sounds like something that might be happening to you, then reading the reminder aloud is a good way of becoming fully aware of what is going on in your mind.

Step 4: Explain the details to someone else.

The next step is to take the reminder to someone you trust so that they can advise you on whether it is right for you or not. This person might be a therapist or counselor, or even a friend or family member, but they must be able to listen and give advice if necessary. It can be helpful to hear things from another person's point of view. They will be able to give you their thoughts on what it means and how they would think about the situation in the future. This person can become your advocate – someone who helps you get out of situations before they cause more harm.

However, when you relate your reminder to a person, they might not be able to work out exactly what the problem is. For example, if you cut yourself to make yourself feel better, then it might be hard for this person to understand why exactly you want to cut yourself. If you tell them everything about the situation, though, including how you were feeling at the time, then they will probably be able to work out what made you react in that way. It is important, however, to remember that this person cannot change your mind or make your feelings go away;

all they can do is give suggestions on how to stop the feelings from getting worse by trying other things.

Mindfulness can also be used in other ways that don't involve meditation or journaling; it is often described as maintaining awareness of what is around you and accepting whatever happens without judgment. It involves taking a step back and realizing that even though something is bothering you, it doesn't mean that there isn't something better happening in the world.

By practicing mindfulness, you will learn that ignoring your feelings isn't always a good thing; if you keep putting off the issue by simply distracting yourself, it will only get worse and might end up negatively affecting your life.

c. Body Awareness Exercises

Body awareness is knowing what is happening in your head and body without having to look at or touch it. The ability of the human body to understand and communicate with itself is astounding. Still, we often ignore these feelings until they become so painful that we cannot ignore them anymore. This exercise helps in identifying your thoughts by developing your inner awareness, which allows your body to tell you what it is feeling. The idea is that by knowing what we are thinking and feeling, we can then work out how to change our thoughts; this is a very useful exercise because it helps us become more in touch with what's inside our heads.

These body awareness exercises are designed to help you develop the ability to be aware of your body. It involves performing any specific action and aiming to identify the emotion you might be experiencing. The main principle is that engaging with your thoughts and feelings through body awareness allows us to understand what we're feeling inside us, enabling us to change these feelings and prevent them from developing into more harmful emotions. These exercises can be used daily.

How to do it:

Step 1: Gently press your feet against the floor.

Start by standing up slowly and placing your feet flat on the floor. Try to feel the pressure of each toe as you stand up and focus on this feeling. If you are feeling dizzy or light-headed, sit back down to ease this sensation so you can fully concentrate on what's happening inside of you. Try to relax your body so you are not holding any tension.

Step 2: Notice which areas of your body feel tense.

Scan your body, starting from your head and moving towards your feet. Consider whether each area feels relaxed. For instance, you might realize that your shoulders and arms don't feel as at ease as the rest of your body. If this is the case, concentrate on relaxing these areas.

Step 3: Engage with your thoughts and feelings.

While doing this exercise, think about an event or situation that has happened. Ask yourself what thoughts have worked their way into your mind like:

- "What am I thinking right now?"

- "What does this mean to me?"

- "What do I think about this situation?"

- "Why am I feeling the way I am feeling?"

- "How is this emotion causing me to feel?"

- "What do I think about how I feel?"

As you are thinking about what happened, try to concentrate on your body again and notice how it feels compared to how it felt before. If you find that your muscles become tenser, focus on relaxing them, from the top down, once again.

Step 4: Practice every day.

This exercise is very useful because it can be done anywhere at any time without any equipment. It is recommended once in the morning and once before going to bed, but you can also have longer sessions if you wish. As you continue to practice the exercise, you will become more aware of your emotions and thoughts, making it much easier to alter them.

This exercise can also be adapted to fit a certain situation; for example, if you are with a friend who you are worried about, you could carry out the exercise with them in mind. Instead of concentrating on what you are thinking and how your body feels, concentrate on them and ask how they feel. If they seem angrier or more stressed than normal, think about what this means and how they feel about you. If you are feeling less stressed, think about what this means and how it makes you feel. This can make you feel more at ease around them, which will enable the two of you to put your worries and concerns behind you.

d. The Body Clock Game

This is another exercise that can be done at anytime, anywhere. This exercise aims to make you more cognizant of your thoughts and feelings, much like the body awareness exercises. Instead of concentrating on your body as one unit, this exercise looks at each part separately so that you can understand what each part of your body is telling you.

The game enables you to identify any changes in your body that occur as a result of your emotions, and it allows you to monitor how your emotions have evolved; this allows for insight through comparison of how you feel from one day to the next.

This exercise is designed to help with developing a sense of awareness, which allows for an understanding of your body and how it is affected by your emotions. You can also do this exercise with other people. In that case, it can be considered a social exercise because you are practicing the ability to understand others, which is a very important part of life.

How to do it:

Step 1: Close your eyes and relax.

Focus on relaxing your body; in particular, try to release any tension you may feel in the area you want to concentrate on. Concentrate on relaxing your muscles one by one and notice how it feels when each area is relaxed.

Step 2: Focus on a specific area.

Next, concentrate on a specific area of your body and think about how it feels compared to how it felt yesterday or the day before. Try comparing this to other areas of your body to see where any changes have been made.

Step 3: Focus on the present moment.

Focus on how that area feels now compared to how it felt pre-viously and notice the feelings that this elicits in your body. Compare this with another area. Do two areas make you feel the same way, or does one make you feel something more than the other?

Step 4: Look at how things change over time.

Think about whether the way you feel today is different from what it used to be, and if it is, then think about where this difference has come from. Try to use your body imaging skills to find an answer as to whether your emotions have developed due to something that has happened since yesterday, or if they have changed for some other reason. This can be thought of as a self-awareness exercise because you are becoming aware of yourself and your emotions through using your body awareness skills. It can help you can learn more about yourself and understand how your emotions change over time.

When finished:

Once you have finished thinking about your feelings, continue what you were doing before the exercise. You should start to feel more stable and aware. Try to learn from this experience to help control your emotions in the future.

This exercise combines the skills of body awareness and self-awareness. It can be used as a self-development exercise because it is about becoming more aware of yourself. You will comprehend your emotions and responses better, enabling you to react appropriately in challenging circumstances.

These mindfulness exercises help you become more aware of how your emotions evolve and can help you find out what triggered a particular emotion in the first place.

2. The Mirroring Method

Another technique that you can use to identify your emotions is the Mirroring Method, which involves finding a person you can mimic. The individual whose emotions you are trying to mimic must be someone with an emotionally expressive face and body – this will help you discover how your emotions change.

There are numerous theories explaining how this method works.

The two most common theories are:

Mimicking Facial Expression

This is based on the idea that if you mimic facial expressions, your emotions will change because you will learn to become aware of your own facial movements. This will help you recognize and control your emotions.

Mimicking Voice

According to this theory, if you mimic someone else's facial expressions while also copying what they're saying, you'll learn more about their feelings and improve your own self-awareness.

By learning to switch between speaking and listening, you may be able to improve your self-awareness skills because it allows you to become more aware of how someone is feeling at any particular moment in time.

How to do it:

Step 1: Find someone to imitate and focus on them.

The first step for this exercise is finding someone you can focus on and mimic. This person should be someone that you are familiar with, such as a friend or family member. They should be someone who is emotionally expressive and someone you feel comfortable around.

Step 2: Think about their emotions.

Once you have found a suitable individual, try to identify what emotions they are feeling and compare with how they generally feel. Think about whether the individual is feeling happy or sad, and think about what might have caused them to feel this way.

Step 3: Begin to mimic their facial expression.

The next step involves beginning to mimic the individual's facial expression. It is helpful to see yourself in a mirror when doing this exercise to check for accuracy when changing your expression. You may also find that your mouth reflects how the other person is feeling.

Step 4: Smile if they are happy and frown if they are sad.

If the person is happy, smile while you are mimicking their facial expressions so that you can learn what a happy face looks like. However, if they are sad, then you should frown while imitating their facial movements because this will make you more aware of what a sad face looks like; it can improve your self-awareness skills at the same time.

Step 5: Alter your expression as necessary.

As you mimic the other person, then try to alter your expression depending on whether their emotions change. If the individual's facial expression changes, you should quickly change your expression to match it.

Step 6: Have fun with it.

As you learn about the different emotions that someone is feeling, try to enjoy the exercise. Observe how you respond to this person and how they express themselves verbally and physically, as well as how you interpret how other people feel. This is a very enjoyable process that will enable you to become even more self-aware.

The Mirroring Method is useful for developing self-awareness because it allows you to become more aware of how someone else is feeling. By mimicking their facial expressions and voice, you can improve your ability to understand how someone else is feeling. This can help you to change your own emotions and therefore gain greater control over them. This exercise can also be used to create a happy or sad mood by simply altering your expression or voice, which will be very useful in the future when communicating with other people.

3. The Voice Dialogue Technique

The Voice Dialogue technique is a psychotherapeutic approach to communication and personal development developed in the 1950s by voice dialogue originator Harry Guntrip. It focuses on communication between the different parts of a person's psyche through dialogues or conversations. The method helps people become more self-aware and can be used as an exercise or a way to improve self-awareness to reduce emotional distress and gain greater control over one's emotions. It is sometimes referred to as "internal family systems."

The Voice Dialogue method is based on object relationships and the assumption that each part of a person's psyche has an internal relationship with another part. These internal relationships stimulate changes in behavior and can be used to provoke psychological change. The voice dialogue approach emphasizes that an unsatisfiable need causes a person's emotional distress and that the mind, emotions, and feelings are interrelated and interactive. According to voice dialogue theory, emotional reactions are sources within interactions with objects in one's environment, such as people, places, or things. When these objects do not satisfy this need, they provoke emotional reactions in people, which stimulate further interactions and create more unsatisfied needs in other objects within the environment, creating more emotional reactions. Voice dialogue theory states that creating emotional reactions is a dynamic, cyclical process of actions and reactions, which can be broken down and changed by conscious intervention.

Voice dialogue theory is based on three fundamental assumptions. These are:

- A person has a "self" or personality, which consists of a collection of subselves (parts within the mind).

- An object in one's environment stimulates feelings by interacting with those subselves.

- People have the ability to alter their emotional responses by altering how they interact with their objects because it is a function of their unconscious mind.

The method can be used to induce change through self-awareness and to reduce emotional distress by confronting the unconscious mind. It is also useful for personal development and can develop self-awareness, self-esteem, confidence, and assertiveness.

How to do it:

Step 1: Creating a Safe Space – Set the Scene

To help you become more self-aware and increase your self-esteem, you must be able to confront the different parts of your personality. The voice dialogue method allows you to do this because it involves conversing with the different parts of yourself. This will allow you to become aware of what each part is feeling and why it feels that way. To do this effectively, find a quiet space where you can be alone and undisturbed.

Consider the following:

- Your garden, your favorite room, your bedroom, your lounge, your balcony. Choose a setting appeals to you!

- Candles are good for setting the atmosphere but if you don't have them around, try using some incense or essential oils instead.

- Soft music and dim lights can help to relax you and get you in the mood for this exercise.

You can practice the voice dialogue exercise anywhere, as long as you're at ease and at ease.

Step 2: The Warm-Up

Starting with some encouraging self-talk is a good way to get yourself in the right frame of mind. This will allow you to focus your thoughts and concentrate on the way you want to feel. The warm-up will also help relax you, making it easier for you to concentrate. Practice this part because, if done well, it will make it easier for you to finish the exercise and will keep you from getting distracted by tension or anxiety.

Consider reciting one of the following mantras to help you relax:

- "I am now in a safe space that is free from distractions. The outside world is shut out, and I am completely focused on listening carefully to my inner dialogue."

- "I deserve to live and to be happy. I have high self-esteem and am proud of who I am."

- "I will do my best, now and in the future."

- "When I want something, I go for it without worrying about what might happen. It is up to me, not for other people, what happens to me."

- "When something goes wrong, it isn't the end of the world – there are thousands of other things in the world that are going right."

- "I can generate many good things in my life if I put my

mind to it."

Take time to think about and write down the things you feel grateful for; this will allow you to focus on what is good in your life, and can help you appreciate the positives!

Step 3: The Dialogue

At this point, you start having conversations with the various facets of your personality. The voice dialogue method helps you become aware of all the different parts of yourself and how they interact. This will help you identify how each part of yourself interacts with the others. It then becomes easier for you to make changes within your personality and improve your ability to deal with challenging situations in the future.

As you are going through the exercise, take a deep breath and focus on each part of your personality, asking:

- **"What is this part of me feeling?"** This will allow you to become aware of why the part might be reacting in the way that they are.

- **"Why is this part of me reacting in this way?"** This will allow you to understand that it may be triggered by something within your mind. If you can identify what triggers these emotions, it will become easier to deal with them in the future.

- **"How can I make this part of me feel happier?"** This can be done by not reacting to the situation impulsively and not worrying about everything that went wrong. Instead, concentrate on what was good about the situation and learn from it.

- **"How will I respond differently next time?"** This question will help you become more aware of how you react to so you can avoid any negative situations or responses from occurring in future.

- **"What are some things that are good about me?"** The more positive stuff there is, the easier it is for me to be happy. This will help to build your self-esteem and not take anything for granted.

- **"What is this part of me thinking?"** This will allow you to become aware of why this part of you might be feeling anxious or concerned about something that has happened in the past.

- **"How can I help this part of me cope better with these negative emotions?"** You'll increase your awareness of your triggers and learn better coping strategies for these feelings. Being honest with yourself makes it possible to deal with any issues that may be causing you problems in life.

- **"How positive can I make myself feel? I want to feel happy."** This will allow you to practice being more positive and developing your skills in this area.

Be patient and don't rush the exercise. There is no right or wrong way to do this exercise, so if you feel unsure, just take a deep breath and continue to talk to yourself until you feel like you have gotten your point across.

It may take some time for these various aspects of yourself to start interacting in a way that is good for you. Practice this exercise regularly; even if you don't feel like doing it, do it anyway because your mind and personality will not change overnight.

Step 4: General Thoughts and Feedback

This is the final step in which you take a break from the exercise, but remind yourself to be patient because it will take time for these changes to fully develop within you. It can be helpful to listen to music that helps you to think positively or watch a movie or video that makes you feel happy or excited. It's also a good idea to write down these thoughts as it can help you to change your attitude and improve your ability to cope with difficult situations in the future.

Regularly review these positive thoughts and feelings that you have written down, as this may give you good ideas for making yourself happier.

This technique is designed to help you to become aware of all the different elements that make up your personality. It will take some time for these different parts of yourself to interact in a way that is positive and helpful, but by following the four steps provided, you can learn more about yourself and improve the way that you feel about life.

Don't worry if you can't remember all the elements of your personality straight away or if some aspects come to the front of your mind and others don't. This exercise is about building awareness and getting to know more about yourself, so any progress that you make is a good thing. This exercise has been designed for you to use over a long period of time, so it's important that you don't rush it.

4. The Intuitive Method

This method of managing your emotions is based on the idea of being more open-minded and going with your first thoughts and feelings. By allowing yourself to experience your feelings and emotions more fully, you can learn more about yourself.

This method is designed to help you become aware that there are many different parts of yourself that you don't need to hide or be ashamed of. By being honest with yourself about what you feel, you can learn more about how the different parts of your personality interact and how they affect the way you feel about life.

It's crucial that you don't use this exercise as an excuse to beat yourself up with unpleasant emotions or thoughts; rather, its goal is to increase your awareness of your personality and promote happiness and self-confidence. If you are honest enough with yourself, it can be possible for you to make the changes that you need to feel better about yourself.

How to do it:

Step 1: Contemplation

Set aside some time to think about yourself and your personality.

Ask yourself the following questions:

Q: How do you feel about yourself?

A: ____

Q: Do you feel like there is more to yourself than what you consciously know?

A: ____

Q: Do you feel like you are the only one who knows what is right for you?

A: ____

Q: What makes you happy, and what makes you sad?

A: ____

Q: Are there any parts of your personality you don't want to talk about or are ashamed of?

A: ____

Q: Do you think differently at different times?

A: ____

Q: Do you have different emotions that you switch between?

A: ____

Q: Does everything around you seem to feel either happy or sad?

A: ____

Q: How do people react to your personality?

A: ____

Q: Do you talk to yourself, or do people talk to you the same way they would talk to another person?

A: ____

Q: What kind of interests do you have, and how do others respond when they find out about them?

A: ____

Q: If something bad happened, would it be a surprise if other people didn't try to help you?

A: ____

Being sincere with yourself will help you better understand how various facets of your personality interact with one another. It's better that you don't move on to the next step until this is the case.

Step 2: Self-Reflection

Once you have completed Step 1, take some time to think about yourself for a while. This will make it easier for you to recognize your thoughts and feelings. Think about how different parts of your personality interact with each other and how they affect how you feel about life and your experiences.

Any thoughts or feelings should be written down, but it's best to limit yourself to one or two at a time, especially if you're not fully aware of what they are. It's a good idea to give each emotion you have some thought so that you can understand it more clearly.

This exercise is not about trying to fix anything or making a decision about how you feel your personality should be; instead, it is designed to help you realize how many different parts of yourself are in play and to make you more aware of these different parts and how they interact with each other. Write your thoughts down so they can be explored during Step 3.

Step 3: Subconscious Identification

This step can be completed in one of two ways; you can either:

- Ask your friends or family members whether they have any ideas about your personality, or;

- Work through a list of the different elements in your personality and try to discover which ones are very important to you and which ones are not so important.

The idea behind this step is to discover which ideas about your personality are important for you to know and which are not as important as others so that you can make changes where necessary.

How to do it:

Step 3.1: Ask your friends and family members

Ask your friends or family members if have any advice about your personality and how it affects the way that people respond to you. Consider why your friends and family members might have these ideas about you. Write down possible answers to these questions.

Step 3.2: Discover which aspects of your personality are important

Consider a list of potential personality traits and decide which ones you are familiar with and which ones you are not. Write down different parts of your personality on pieces of paper so that the words can be spread out on the table in front of you, allowing you to see them all at once.

To better understand your own personality, consider:

- The way you talk to others

- The way you feel about things

- The way that things affect you

- How others react to your personality

- How you are affected when people respond differently to how you would expect

- What makes you feel sad, and what makes you feel happy

- What makes you feel uncomfortable and what doesn't

- What makes you want to do things and what stops you from doing things

- How people respond to your ideas

- What makes you feel relaxed and what makes you feel stressed

- How others react when you are happy, sad, or angry

Take some time thinking about each of these questions as this will help you to focus on the different parts of your personality that might be causing problems for you. Every time an idea or feeling comes to mind, you write it down.

Step 4: Confirmation and Re-Evaluation

When you have finished writing down all of the parts of your personality, read all the different thoughts and feelings that came to mind so you can examine them in more detail.

The questions below might help you with this step:

Q: What do I think about each of these ideas?

A: ____

Q: Are there any parts of my personality that I find important? Why are they important to me?

A: ____

Q: How much do I think about these parts of myself?

A: ____

It's a good idea to read through the different ideas you have written down and spend some time thinking about the ones you identify as important.

Step 5: Trial Period to Redefine Your Ideas About Your Personality

It's important that this trial period is thought of as very easy and that you don't put too much pressure on yourself to change immediately.

Consider each of the various facets of your personality throughout the trial period and determine whether it is necessary for you to alter these facets. It's best if there are no other major changes taking place in your life during this period.

Step 6: Reflection of True Personality and Analysis of Changes

Make an effort to ascertain whether or not you perceive yourself differently after the trial period because doing so will allow you to pinpoint the cause of the changes. Write down any changes that have taken place and think about where these changes came from; it's also good to mark the date the change occurred in a diary so you can remember it.

When you have re-examined your changes and any new ideas that have come to mind, write down all of the ideas that come to mind on different pieces of paper so that they are spread out in front of you. Place these ideas in two groups called "Old Ideas" and "New Ideas"; this will help you to separate your old ideas from the newer ideas that come to mind.

It's important that your new ideas are thought of as just that, new ideas, and that they don't get mixed up with the old ideas; otherwise, it might be hard for you to tell which changes have taken place as a result of Step 5 and which have taken place as a result of something else.

Step 7: Evaluation of New Ideas About Your Personality

Spend some time considering each of your new insights into who you are. It's possible that you may disagree with any of the things you have written down and would like to change them in some way. If you do agree with your new thoughts, it might be that you want to keep them as part of yourself, but if not, you can choose to change them in some way.

If you disagree with any of the things you've written down, it's a good idea to explain why you don't think those things are significant and why you feel that way. Reviewing all the concepts that were noted during this step is a good idea. If they seem to be variations on a single concept, think about these concepts all at once and see if you can isolate a unifying concept or theme.

Writing down your fresh concepts will ensure that you always have access to them. This might also motivate you to think back on them and consider whether anything has changed since the trial period.

It's also a good idea to ask someone to check over your ideas with you; they might notice something that you did not.

Step 8: Continued Evaluation of New Ideas

Continue thinking about your new ideas over the next few days to make sure that you still agree with them. If, for some reason, you no longer agree with any of your ideas, write down why this happened, as it might give you some idea about what changes have occurred since Step 3. Spend a few hours each day reading through any new thoughts that have come to mind during the trial period. Continue this process for at least a few days.

This is quite a lengthy process and might take up two or three weeks of your time, depending on how much change you wish to make, but it is important not to rush through this process as it won't pick up any subtle changes that might have taken place since Step 3.

It is a good idea to check back on your new ideas regularly; after these few weeks, your new thoughts should begin to become more solid.

These steps are designed so that your personality can change in such a way that it reflects your true nature and shows what changes you should make in your life.

You must follow these instructions for a few days or weeks, but once you get into the habit, the process should come quite naturally.

The methods mentioned here should be easy to follow and use; they are based on psychological techniques that have been used to help people with their mental problems. It is important to realize that you might need further help if you find it hard to follow these method; as such, please seek the advice of a professional if you are in any doubt about the process.

You might find it hard to make changes in yourself, but if you have reached this point, then you have already made some important steps towards making changes in your life and recognizing what these changes should be.

CHAPTER 5: DECIDING TO ACT ON OUR EMOTIONS

Acting on our emotions doesn't always serve us well, as we're wired to act in certain ways, regardless of how irrational they are. There are many ways to act on our emotions. This chapter will help you figure out how to act on your emotions wisely so that you can make changes in your life.

It is important to understand that acting on one's emotions does not always mean rushing into something without thinking about it well enough first. We have all made bad decisions before; we have all experienced situations that make us wish we had paid more attention to the long-term consequences of our actions.

Failing to Act on Negative Emotions

Negative emotions can be very powerful; some emotions are so strong that we often find it difficult to even think about what action we should take in response. This is especially true of many negative emotions such as anger and frustration. Often, these feelings are accompanied by blocked thoughts, and our ability to think is greatly reduced, making us act strangely.

Reasons Why We Don't Act on Emotions

When we are experiencing particularly strong emotions, it can be challenging to understand why we don't act on them. However, there are several reasons for this:

1. Belief in What Others Think of Us

Many people don't act on their emotions because they feel it will make them look weak in the eyes of others; the truth is that the people who we consider "strong" often do not act on their emotions. Most people are too self-conscious to show how their emotions influence their actions and are afraid that they will appear foolish.

Humans are social creatures; as such, we have a natural desire to belong to and be accepted by groups and communities. If we act on our emotions and put ourselves out there, people might see us as a threat. Instead of acting on our emotions, many people will hide them behind their behavior; they will pretend that they have control over themselves and that their feelings do not influence their actions. When this happens, they gain acceptance and become part of the group. The few individuals who act on their emotions often find themselves rejected and ostracized from society.

2. Lack of Feedback

Determining whether we are acting in a new way or if we are just repeating our old behavior can be difficult at times. People prefer to believe that they are unique and special; they dislike the notion that they may be unknowingly repeating mistakes. This is especially true if our emotions were at the forefront of our actions – we can often forget whether or not our actions were intentional or just a response to an emotional stimulus.

People often think that they are acting in an informed and appropriate way; however, it can be quite difficult to predict how other people react to our actions. Unfortunately, we can never be sure how others will feel about what we do or say to them. Even if our actions seem inappropriate to us, there is no guarantee that others will find them so – this will only be the case if there is an obvious problem with our behavior. We need to examine our actions and stress test them before we make any assumptions about how other people will react.

3. Fear of Change and of Being Wrong

It can sometimes be difficult to risk acting on our emotions, especially if we fear change. Many fear acting in a way that might be new and different because they feel this may be a sign that they are making some mistake. This is seen in the behavior toward new ideas; many people will resist any idea or action which could lead to change for fear that it might not work out as well as they hoped – this often stems from the fear of being wrong. Additionally, there is frequently a fear of change that may result in the desire to maintain the status quo.

If we lack self-esteem, then this fear of being wrong can also prevent us from acting on our emotions. There will always be some level of risk attached to any decision. We cannot avoid making mistakes; however, we can minimize the chances of making them by being honest with ourselves and ensuring that we are ready to accept the consequences of our actions.

4. Fear of Being Authentic

Some people worry that they will appear too vulnerable if they act on their emotions; these people will often put on a front to distance themselves from the way that they truly feel. Unfortunately, not being honest with how we feel can lead to us doing things that are detrimental to our physical and mental health. It is normal to experience anger, frustration, and agitation; we should not be embarrassed to express these feelings to the world. It can often be difficult to accept that our behavior can affect our emotions, and vice versa, especially if we are used to hiding behind a mask of deceit.

It is important to remember that it is never wrong to have feelings that we don't understand. When this happens, we need to think about our emotions using the techniques from the previous chapter; this will help us become more conscious of them and understand why we act the way we do.

5. Fear of Taking Responsibility for Our Actions

We should always take responsibility for how we act and how it affects other people, but this can sometimes cause anxiety. We should always hold ourselves truly responsible for how we deal with the situations we face.

Many people will go to great lengths to avoid taking responsibility for their actions; they want to believe that they are innocent in all situations, and they want others to take responsibility for their own emotions and actions. However, we alone must accept our responsibility for how we treat others and act. We should be able to see how these things affect other people or us and learn from our mistakes.

6. Fear of Abandonment

Most people have experienced rejection by others; this can often lead to a feeling of abandonment. We might lose a friend or a romantic partner, which makes us feel lonely and sad; this can sometimes cause us to avoid socializing with other people, leaving us very uncomfortable in new environments. Unfortunately, we may avoid people who could become very good friends or partners. There are other ways that this fear of abandonment can manifest, though it frequently results in the sense of loneliness. Instead of avoiding relationships with other people, we might engage in destructive or inappropriate relationships to avoid feeling lonely. This can often lead to personal destruction or exploitation; we may start to feel dependent on others and afraid of being alone. In reality, we are usually the only ones who can make ourselves feel lonely by putting others before ourselves.

We need to learn that it is never wrong to feel lonely; this is a normal part of being human, and everyone goes through it at some stage. It is important not to let this fear of abandonment stop us from learning how to be happy and content with our own company; acting on these emotions might make us more confident. Similarly, we should not avoid socializing with other people just because we fear rejection.

These issues can be very difficult to overcome; negative emotions often greatly affect our actions. They can make us feel weak and vulnerable, and as though we are at their mercy.

Techniques for Acting on Our Emotions

Knowing what to do when feeling negative emotions is extremely important. It is important to remember that it is never wrong to feel the way we do – however, negative emotions aren't always helpful.

The following are some of the techniques we can use to respond in a positive way to our emotions:

1. Softening the Skin

When feeling a negative emotion, it is important to remember that it is never wrong to feel the way we do. However, negative emotions often cause us to act in ways that are not helpful. This technique helps you feel less afraid by accepting how you feel and eliminating the negative aspects of your emotions. Softening the skin helps you to feel more comfortable in your body and allows you to accept how you feel without worrying about the consequences of these feelings.

There are several reasons why this technique can be so helpful:

- The first is that it helps you to feel less afraid of your emotions; you can acknowledge that they are a part of you. You will no longer be afraid of your emotions' negative aspects; instead, you will be able to experience your emotions without fear of being exposed or vulnerable. Instead, you will learn to accept yourself for who you are and make decisions based on your true feelings rather than what other people want you to do.

- Secondly, the softening skin technique helps you to be more gentle with yourself. Because we are less afraid of the negative aspects of our emotions, we start accepting ourselves for who we are and make decisions based on what is best for us. When we are feeling vulnerable or exposed, we tend to act on our emotions and take different actions than we would have otherwise.

- Finally, this technique helps you develop self-compassion. This is when you are kind and accepting towards yourself when you feel sad or hurt rather than being harsh with yourself because of how you feel; this allows us to start to accept these parts of ourselves while avoiding the negative aspects that they contain.

Softening the skin can be a great way to respond to negative emotions.

How to do it?

Step 1: Soften

Start by choosing an arm or leg and noticing how tense it is. Tighten the arm, release it and imagine that tension leaving your body. Once you do this with one limb, move on to another until every part has been relaxed. You can do the same with your stomach and chest. Once you have done this, you will start to feel more at ease and in touch with how you feel.

Step 2: Breathe

Now that your body is relaxed, move on to your breathing. Find somewhere comfortable to sit or lie down and take a few deep breaths in through your nose and out through your mouth. Take responsibility for how you feel by acknowledging that you are the only one who can make yourself feel calm. Remember that it is not necessary to control your breathing; instead, you should focus on how it makes you feel when you inhale and exhale.

Step 3: Feel

Now all that is left is your emotions. Spend as much time as is necessary concentrating on your current feelings. Accept the way you feel and do not judge yourself for feeling this way; instead, pay attention to what the emotion feels like and think about the root of the emotion (the memory, thought, or belief that causes the emotion). Soak this in for a few minutes before gently returning your focus to your body.

Step 4: Gently return

The next step is to bring your attention back to your body gently. As you breathe normally, use one of your hands to touch yourself; focus on how the warmth of your skin feels against your hand or the floor. After that, slowly open your eyes and scan the space for recognizable items. Now that you are more aware of yourself, begin to appreciate how accepting you are towards yourself and all of those parts that make up who you are. You can learn to recognize your kindness and self-compassion by recognizing that the negative parts of yourself are not inherently bad; this allows you to feel more at ease and in touch with how you truly feel.

This technique can help you to act in response to your emotions because it helps you to recognize that your emotions are part of you, not something that you have no control over. When you are at the mercy of your emotions, you can feel weak and vulnerable. However, when you can recognize them as a part of you that you can choose to act in response to, they will no longer hold as much power over you.

2. The Jiggling Ball Technique

This technique is helpful with anger. Anger often makes us feel out of control and puts us into fight-or-flight mode; our rational thinking and self-control are turned off, and we react to what is happening around us. This can be extremely detrimental as we will act in ways that are not helpful and can make many mistakes in the process. Making decisions based on logic rather than acting out of rage can be greatly aided by learning how to control our anger.

The jiggling ball technique is a calming technique that can help us to control our anger and heal any damage we may have caused by acting on it.

How to do it:

Step 1: Relax

Sit comfortably on the floor, place one hand over your heart, and the other over your stomach. Inhale deeply through your nose, followed by a slow mouth exhalation. Relaxing your body and allow it to sway aimlessly from side to side. As you do this, pay attention to the feelings in each part of your body; how does this part feel? Is there tension, or is there some other feeling going on? Spend as much time as you need paying attention to the way your body feels before returning to a more relaxed state.

Step 2: The ball

Determine whereabouts in the body your anger is focused. For example, when you were a child and were angry with your parent over something, that feeling was most likely focused on your stomach because this is often the part of the body that feels pain the most. Now imagine a small ball inside that part of you that has been silently and gently filled with this deep-seated anger.

Ask yourself these questions:

- Does the ball feel as if it is getting bigger and bigger?

- How heavy does it feel inside of you?

- Is the anger coming off it so powerful that you can almost taste it in your mouth?

- Can you see any redness on your body?

- Does it move that quickly, or is it moving slowly and steadily?

- Can you feel the anger leaving your body?

As you ask these questions, pay close attention to how the ball feels. Pay close attention to how much it vibrates and how heavy it feels inside of you. Gently sway back and forth as if a small wind was coming off your entire being. As you're doing this, you will start to feel a change in the energy surrounding you, and all of that anger will begin to disappear. The ball will start to feel lighter and smaller; it will get warmer and warmer, your body will start to calm down again and feel relaxed, and you will be filled with love and kindness towards yourself.

Step 3: Letting it go

Do this until the ball feels so light you could let it go. Then imagine that the ball inside you is shrinking in size; feel as if it is no longer vibrating until it feels completely calm. Once the ball has become minuscule, let it go. Focus on your breathing again;

take some more deep breaths to fully bring this new calm and peaceful energy back into your body.

This technique can be performed when any anger arises.

3. The Deep Breathing Technique

This technique is designed to help us to become calm and feel more at ease in situations where we feel anxious or upset. It can also help us relax when stressed out, allowing our hearts and minds to feel lighter and happier.

It works by helping us to breathe in a way that deeply soothes our nervous system, slowing down the heart rate, lowering blood pressure and eliminating cravings for stimulants.

Also, deep breaths create a calming effect on the brain via the pituitary gland. However, when someone has depression or is anxious, their nervous system can become overly stimulated and overworked, leading to feelings of overwhelming anxiety or depression.

How to do it:

Step 1: Setting the Stage

Locate a quiet place where you can spend some time alone without being bothered by others. To help you feel more at ease, light some candles or turn down the lights. Get comfortable in your seat, and sit up straight with your shoulders back and head held high as if you were walking into a powerful meeting. Close your eyes for two to three minutes and focus on how it feels when you are sitting in this position. Allow yourself to experience any emotions that arise, whether they are constructive feelings of calmness or unsettling negative emotions, and then concentrate on calmly breathing through them until they pass. Take a deep breath in through your nose and exhale through your mouth.

Step 2: The Breathing

Now breathe into the area of your stomach around the back of your ribs by the spine. Feel as if there were two large balloons on either side of you; blow air into them as if keeping time to a song. Take a deep breath in through your nose, filling up those balloons as much as possible, and exhale it back out through your nose again. Do this for as long as you need to, taking deep breaths and exhaling until you feel completely relaxed.

Step 3: The Feeling

Consider how it feels to breathe deeply. Focus on the calmness that breathing in deep brings you, the happy sensation of being relaxed, and the peace that comes from this. Focus on what it feels like not to have any tension or discomfort inside of you anymore; focus all your attention on how good it feels to be able to do this. If you become distracted by outside thoughts or other feelings, return your focus to taking these deep breaths, allowing them to calm you.

Step 4: Letting Go

Your breathing should have calmed down by now, and your body should have relaxed and become more at ease. Gently open your eyes. Remind yourself how satisfying it is to be able to maintain your focus on your relaxed, easy breathing, allowing your inner joy to emerge naturally.

This technique can be used anytime you feel anxious, worried, or upset.

When you are lying in bed, ready to sleep at night, try the deep breathing technique to ease yourself into a more relaxed state of mind. You can also try this at work, before going shopping or when going home after work; as long as you find a quiet place, this practice will be effective.

4. The Swinging Pendulum Technique

A pendulum is a weight on the end of a string that moves back and forth in a circular motion based on the pull of gravity. This motion is caused by the weight's inertia. The force of gravity will eventually transfer this motion into a circular path, with the pendulum moving in a full circle over time.

The swinging pendulum technique works by bringing our attention to the area of our heart and letting us feel its gentle rhythms. In doing so, we become focused solely on how our heart feels at that moment, letting go of all other thoughts and feelings that may distract us.

How can this help?

Our heart has a natural rhythm like the swinging pendulum, with a slight pause before each beat, where it fills with blood. If we can feel this "resting period" within our heart, it will help us to slow down and focus better; this helps us to function more easily, as we can focus on the task at hand instead of being distracted by stress or worry.

How to do it?

Step 1: Describe the Movement

Find a quiet place to sit and wait for your mind to "rest." Imagine a pendulum swinging back and forth. Describe the way this pendulum swings gently as it moves back and forth in a full circle around itself. Doing this will help to relax your mind, letting go of other thoughts and feelings about the day.

Step 2: Listen to Your Heartbeat

Next, bring your attention to the way your heart feels. Place one hand on your chest and focus on the rhythm of your heartbeat.

Notice the slight pause between beats; this should feel very similar to the swinging of a pendulum. Let go of all other thoughts and feelings in your mind.

Now focus on your breathing again, noticing how it feels as you inhale and exhale. Let the rhythm of your heart relax you, letting go of all thoughts and feelings that may be distracting you from the present moment.

Do this for a few minutes returning to your everyday life.

The swinging pendulum technique allows you to concentrate better and feel more relaxed; by bringing your mind and body into the present moment, it will allow you to let go of any other distracting thoughts or feelings you may have.

5. The Hands Technique

Do you ever find yourself wanting to do something, but your hands just don't want to cooperate? This is exactly why the hands technique was invented. The hands technique uses our hands in a way that allows us to stay focused on the task at hand while bypassing any nervousness that may be plaguing us.

How can this help?

When we are feeling nervous, our hands can become incredibly distracting. This makes it difficult for us to focus on anything other than the way our hands feel. The anxiety caused by this keeps us from focusing on anything else, making it difficult to function in daily life.

How to do it:

Step 1: Relax

When doing this technique, sit down and close your eyes. Let go of all thoughts and feelings about the task at hand, freeing yourself from any pressure that may have been creating mental clutter.

Step 2: Listen to Your Hands

Next, bring your attention to your hands. Focus on how they feel as they rest, and describe it in your mind. Now, let go of all other thoughts and feelings, and begin slowly moving your hands alongside one another. Focus on how they feel as they move slowly together or apart. Try not to control them. Instead, use the natural movement of your hands as a way to relax; this will help remove any tension that may be lurking within you.

Now focus on your breathing, noticing how it feels as you inhale and exhale. Let the movement of your hands relax you, letting go of all thoughts and feelings that may be distracting you from the present moment.

The hands method can allow you to focus inwards and gain perspective, especially when feeling nervous.

Negative emotions can have a significant impact on our lives, causing us to be unable to function normally. They can affect our memory, concentration, and our ability to focus. All in all, these emotions can throw us off balance and make it very difficult to live our lives.

The techniques described above are excellent ways for you to improve your self-control. You will feel more in control of your life and be better able to concentrate on yourself by using these techniques, which are an essential component of leading a normal life.

These techniques are best learned with guidance; if you are unsure about how they work or would like more information on how they can improve your life, consider consulting a trained psychologist or therapist.

Other Ways You Can Act on Your Emotions

There are other ways in which you can act on your negative emotions. The following are some of the common ones:

1. Distracting Yourself

Distraction is another great tool for acting on emotions. When we feel a negative emotion, it can be difficult to focus on anything other than how we feel; however, distractions can help us stay positive and happy without forcing ourselves to act against what we feel. For instance, it might be beneficial to divert our attention from our feelings of sadness or hurt by engaging in conversation with others or reading a book. However, if we are angry or upset, that might make the situation worse; in this situation, it might be better to distract ourselves by taking a walk or doing something else that makes us feel good but does not involve the person who upset us in the first place.

Positive distractions are activities that we enjoy and benefit from daily. These include things like going for a walk, watching TV, or listening to music. The idea is to find ways in which you can distract yourself by doing something that makes you feel good; avoid focusing on negative emotions by choosing an activity that makes you happy and more relaxed. Allowing yourself to dwell on your negative emotions will only make them seem stronger and more disruptive. Pay attention to something else instead.

Consider what type of distraction would be useful when you are upset or angry at someone or something in your life; then use that distraction whenever you have a bad feeling. If one type of distraction is not working for you, try another until you find an activity that works for you.

2. Talking to Someone

Talking to someone can be one of the most effective ways of handling our emotions. Talking to someone can help you come up with solutions and advice that make it easier for you to respond to how you feel. Sometimes you need a little help or guidance to deal with negative emotions in a healthy way. Talking helps you by giving your emotional brain some direction so that you do not have to struggle as much with your feelings. When you're upset, it can be challenging to decide what will be best for you and those around you, making it hard to know how to react. Speaking to a friend or relative can make it easier for you to act on your feelings in an appropriate way and can make you feel better afterward.

Factors to Consider When Talking to Someone

a. How much do you trust this person?

We may not trust our friends or family members as much as we trust ourselves, but if a friend or relative understands us, they will be able to help us. However, if your family member does not act like they understand you and respond as they should, consider talking to someone else.

b. How much does this person understand you?

While it is important that the person you talk to understands you, it is also important that they have experience dealing with similar problems. If someone has been through similar situations, they may be better able to understand what you are going through and will be able to give you advice on how best to deal with what is troubling you. For example, if a family member has experienced grief due to the loss of a loved one, they may be able to help you if you are facing a similar situation. However, if they have not experienced grief firsthand, they may not know how best to respond. When you are struggling, it can be difficult to know what to do, but talking to someone who is aware of your issues may provide you with the support you need.

c. How clear are your emotions?

If your emotions are very intense, try speaking with someone more emotionally stable than yourself. If you are both emotional, you may get nothing useful out of the conversation. Choose to speak with someone who is cool and collected when speaking, and who will encourage you to express yourself clearly.

d. How much do you want to talk about this?

People frequently feel as though they have no choice but to talk about what is bothering them; however, talking about how we feel when we do not want to will only make us feel worse. Consider how important it is for you to deal with the issue and let your feelings guide your actions. In some cases, talking about the situation may only make things more difficult.

Talking to someone can help you act on your emotions effectively and improve things. If your emotions are keeping you from doing what you need to do, try talking to someone about the issue that is bothering you; your friend or relative may be able to give you some helpful advice or a piece of information that can help you deal with how you feel so that, in the end, it turns out all right.

3. Do Nothing

Doing nothing and just observing your emotions can be a positive thing because it will give you the chance to figure out what you feel and why. In addition, doing nothing will allow your feelings to run their course, and it may turn out that they are not as serious as they might seem. In the long run, you may find that doing nothing is the best action for dealing with your emotions; however, be aware that this is not always the case.

Situations Where Doing Nothing is Good

There are situations when doing nothing is more beneficial rather than acting on your emotions. These include:

a. When you are upset about something that is not a big deal

If you are upset by something minor, there is no reason for you to panic; you will likely feel better just by doing nothing and allowing your feelings to flow. When we are upset about something that is not a big deal, doing nothing can help us feel better in the long run.

b. When you are upset because you could have handled things better

Sometimes we realize that what has happened was not as bad as we thought and that we were doing somewhat poorly at handling the situation; when this happens, it can be a good idea for you to stay calm and get your emotions back under control before talking about it again.

c. When you are upset because you are doing something wrong

Sometimes we feel upset because we are doing something wrong, and this feeling makes us feel bad; however, if what we have done is not too serious, there is no need to worry about it. Rather than trying to fix the problem right away, it is better to ignore it and wait for it to go away. Sometimes, taking a break from the matter can help us figure out how to handle the problem better next time.

d. When you are upset because someone is bothering you

If we are upset about people doing something to us, it can be helpful for us to get over it and have a good time doing something else; if we keep worrying about what has happened, we may end up making things worse by overreacting.

Deciding to act on your emotions or not is important because it will affect your life; however, it can be good to understand how to better handle your emotions before making a decision. Either way, you should do what is right for you, and find a way to deal with the situation appropriately; whether this means dealing with your feelings, talking to someone your trust, or doing nothing depends on the situation.

CHAPTER 6: ACCEPTING YOUR EMOTIONS WITHOUT JUDGEMENT

E motions, whether negative or positive, are something you can learn to accept, even if you do not like them. After all, negative emotions are a part of life. You can also accept positive emotions because they make us feel good, and this feeling is what life is all about. It is okay to feel certain feelings, but it is not okay to judge your feelings.

This chapter is about learning to accept your emotions without judging them as good or bad.

Advantages in Accepting your Emotions Without Judging Them

There are many advantages to accepting your emotions without judging them; however, some of the most important ones are:

1. You learn to accept yourself for who you are

When you judge your feelings, you are judging yourself for having them. On the other hand, when you accept your feelings as they are, it will make you stronger. Accepting your emotions without judging them will make you feel better about yourself, no matter what the situation is.

Accepting yourself for who you are will not just make you feel strong; it will also help you like yourself and know that you are a good person. You might become unsure of who you are and whether your feelings are correct or incorrect when you judge yourself based on what you believe other people want from you. This can make you think that the way you feel is wrong, even when the feeling is natural. Conversely, accepting your feelings without judging them will open up a new world of possibilities, letting you know that it is okay to be the way you are.

2. You will be more comfortable with who you are

When you know it is okay to feel the way you do, you will be more comfortable with yourself and your emotions. Being comfortable with yourself and the natural "you" will make you feel happier because it will remind you that no matter what anyone else says, your emotions are okay, and that is all that matters.

When you feel this way, your true personality will come out in all of your actions. In other words, you will be acting like the kind of person you are inside. Accepting your emotions without judging them will help you stay true to who you really are and will make you feel good about yourself.

3. It will help you accept the world around you

Accepting your emotions without judging them will help you accept the world around you. This can help you take in all your experiences as a whole and not as pieces you have to categorize. Doing this will encourage you to meet new people and try new things.

The world becomes your classroom when you accept yourself for who you are; however, this can also be a place of disappointment when you expect something from someone they don't have. When you accept yourself without judgment and learn to accept the world around you, it will give you the freedom to be your true self. It will open up a new world for yourself that you may have thought impossible.

4. You can look at all the possibilities life has to offer and not just judge them by their cover

When you learn to accept your emotions without judging them, it will help you do things that you never thought that you would do. When you judge your feelings, it limits what your emotions are capable of doing; however, when you stop judging them and accept them for what they are, this opens up a whole new world for you.

Stopping judging yourself and accepting your emotions will make it possible for you to look at all the possibilities life has to offer.

5. You will be less stressed

People who judge themselves for their emotions are hard on themselves and can get pretty upset over things that may not even be that serious; however, once you stop judging your feelings and accept them for what they are, you will be less stressed. Stop judging yourself so that your feelings can do what they were meant to do without you feeling guilty about it.

Once you stop judging your emotions and accept them for what they are, it will make it possible for you to feel good about yourself. This positive thinking is less stressful than the negative thinking that goes on when you judge your emotions; when you accept the way you feel, there will be no reason to think negatively about anything because your true emotions can shine through without you feeling guilty or scared of being judged by someone else.

6. You stop judging other people

When you learn to accept your emotions without judging them, it will also help you be less judgmental towards others. If someone is upset or angry, you will be able to accept the way they feel without feeling that they are wrong. When you stop being judgmental and open your mind, it will be easier for you to understand that they have a reason to feel the way they do, even if you don't agree with what is happening.

It may not always be easy to accept how others are feeling when we don't agree with them; however, when we understand their feelings and know that these feelings are valid for them, it will help us become more compassionate individuals.

Your understanding of how everything in life serves a purpose will become clearer as a result. However, we cannot see this purpose until we learn to stop judging ourselves and other people based solely on our feelings. When you open your mind and stop judging yourself and others based on how you feel, you can bring out the best in everyone by showing them that it is acceptable to be different without fear of judgment.

7. You will be less afraid of new experiences and people

When you stop judging yourself, it will allow you to be open to new experiences and people. Once you learn to accept your emotions, you will no longer be afraid of things you used to. In addition, once other people see that it is okay for them to be different to you, they will also be less afraid of new experiences because they won't feel judged.

Learning how to accept your emotions without judging yourself is a difficult lesson. Still, accepting the way you feel will make it easier to stop being afraid of the unknown.

8. You can see that life has its reasons for everything

When you learn how to accept your emotions without judging yourself, it can help you realize that life always has a valid reason for everything that happens, even if we don't understand it at the time. If we let go of judging our feelings and accept them for what they are, we will be able to see things in a completely new way.

Although you may still not understand why certain things happen, you can see that there is a reason behind everything that occurs because once you stop judging yourself and the world around you, your intuition will create an understanding that may not have been possible before. Learning to accept your emotions without judging them will open up a new way of thinking that is less judgmental and more open-minded.

Learning to accept your emotions without judging yourself will help you see the world from a whole new perspective. You will be able to see the many reasons for why life happens the way it does and how we can live in a less judgmental way towards others and ourselves.

It may take some time before you begin to recognize the advantages of this way of thinking. However, once you learn how to accept your emotions without judging them, this will change many aspects of your life and make it possible for you to live a more fulfilling life.

Techniques for Accepting Emotions Without Judgement

There are a number of different techniques that can help us accept our emotions without judging them. Each can help us to be more understanding of ourselves. Some of these techniques are:

1. The "This Too Shall Pass" Technique

When we judge our emotions, it causes us to feel uncomfortable. However, when we remove this judgment of the emotion and accept it for what it is, it becomes easier for us to move through the emotion without it causing any discomfort.

This allows us not to be frightened or anxious about unfamiliar emotions and to give them their proper time instead of trying hard to get rid of them. When you learn how the "This Too Shall Pass" technique works, you can stop judging your emotions and start accepting them for what they are, so they become less frightening.

Sometimes, all we need is to believe that the emotion will pass and learn to accept it for what it is. This allows us to be open and less judgmental of our emotions, which may allow us to move toward a more fulfilling life.

How and When to Use the "This Too Shall Pass" Technique:

- When you notice that your emotions are becoming too strong and want them to stop, tell yourself out loud, "This too shall pass." Say this until you start to believe it and feel different.

- Start telling yourself that the emotion will pass before it gets too strong. Tell yourself this when the emotion starts, and then tell yourself again at several points during its stay. Tell yourself that this emotion will pass through you when you first notice something changing within your feelings or thoughts, as well as when all of the changes are complete.

- Don't think in time frames or dates. Instead, think of the emotion as a wave that will come and go through you. When you look at your emotions in this way, you will become willing to accept them for what they are without judging them.

- Tell yourself that this emotion is just a wave, and it is nothing more than that. It will come and go through you; however, it will not do any harm. Accept it without judgment or criticism of yourself or the emotion itself.

- Tell yourself that it's okay to feel the way you do, and there is no need to judge it or put on a brave face.

- Remember that you have experienced this emotion before. If you experience a new emotion, allow yourself to accept it as part of the learning process that will help you in the future.

- Talk to friends and family about how your emotions make you feel and see if they can help you understand what they are or why they are there. It can be helpful to know that others feel emotions in the same way we do.

- Remember that emotions are a part of life, and you will be able to accept your emotions as they come and go.

This technique may not be easy at first; however, if you keep a strong belief in yourself and the way your emotions are supposed to change through you – even if you don't know why – it will be a lot easier for you to accept them instead of judging them. This may help you move toward a more fulfilling life that doesn't involve fear or pain.

2. The "Let It Happen" Technique

The "Let It Happen" method, also known as "deliberate acceptance," is a component of Acceptance and Commitment Therapy (ACT), a thorough, empirically supported psychological intervention that also includes mindfulness instruction. According to ACT, the purpose of acceptance (of thoughts, feelings, and bodily sensations) is not to attain a particular mental state or to suppress one's emotions or thoughts but instead to develop the skill of observing them without placing judgments upon them. The aim is to influence rather than change the way one feels.

According to ACT, acceptance is an emotion-focused response that involves accepting all of one's thoughts and feelings rather than judging them and trying to change them (e.g., by suppressing or repressing them). This differs from cognitive-behavioral methods, which tend to focus on changing or eliminating thoughts and feelings. ACT also distinguishes acceptance from resignation ("giving in"). This latter response occurs when one does not adapt to a situation within one's ability, even though it would be beneficial for the individual to do so.

ACT differs from existing cognitive-behavioral therapies in that it teaches acceptance of thoughts and feelings as they are, rather than changing or replacing them with new and desired ones. Acceptance should not be confused with passivity because the ACT emphasizes the highly active and skilled nature of useful life.

It involves:

- Accepting rather than fighting against the fact that difficult thoughts and feelings are present at any moment; is considered fundamental to psychological flexibility (the ability to change one's behavior by choice) – when one reacts unaccepting to thoughts/feelings, they tend to become more intense.

- Separating thoughts and feelings from harmful behaviors; for example, separating the thought of a cigarette from actually smoking a cigarette

- Focusing on values – recognizing important beliefs, memories, and personal sources of strength/hope to cope with difficult experiences effectively

- Directed attention – choosing to actively attend to one's present-moment experience rather than drifting off into worry or fantasy (i.e. mindfulness)

- Value-based action – living one's life in a way consistent with personal values.

ACT recognizes no clear boundaries between thoughts, feelings, and actions.

The Let It Happen technique is best tried out with a simple thought or feeling, before progressing to the more lucid ones. You may need some time to realize how helpful the technique is, so you should only apply it occasionally. Furthermore, even though it might seem prudent to test out this technique on larger issues at first, it is typically simpler to start with smaller issues.

How to Use the "Let It Happen" Technique:

- If a thought or feeling comes into your head, allow it to be there without judgment.

- Try and let go of how you think you should feel about what is occurring and allow yourself to accept the thought or feeling for what it is (i.e., is it a good or bad thought or feeling, is it a thought or feeling I would choose to have, is this what I would want my life to look like right now, etc.)

How can you do this:

- Don't overthink it. Just let it happen. If you don't allow yourself to feel enough, you will never be able to feel anything at all.

- Remain aware of your feelings.

- Don't fight it or try to make it go away. It will naturally dissipate if you accept it.

- Feel the feeling! Be in the moment, be in the now, and don't escape into something you hope might make you feel better, like drinking, eating, or taking drugs.

- Stay present and aware of your feelings, no matter how difficult they may be.

- Don't analyze the feeling or think about what meaning it might have for you. Just observe it and allow yourself to be with it for however long it is there.

- Don't judge the feeling and certainly don't judge yourself for having the feeling (i.e., don't say, "I shouldn't feel this way because....this should be different in my life right now...etc.).

- Don't go into future thinking (i.e., worrying about things that could happen) or past thinking (i.e., remembering other things that have happened).

- Observe your bodily sensations and don't judge them as good or bad. If you feel tension, be present with it without trying to make it go away. If you feel tired, observe that with acceptance and don't judge yourself for feeling that way or try to force yourself into being more energetic.

- Relax into whatever may be happening (for example, if someone is talking to you or something happens in front of you that causes tension, observe how you feel in response instead of trying to change what is happening).

- Don't beat yourself up for not being able to control everything all the time.

- Accepting that your real life may not be what you had anticipated will be helpful here. Don't try to force yourself into being someone you are not and don't live your life for other people.

- If something does happen that makes you feel bad (like someone says something cruel or mean to you), accept that this has happened without judging it. Remember, our lives are not perfect, and we can only do our best with all that is in our control at any given moment. Sometimes, how we react to whatever is happening in our lives is the only thing we can control.

- Try to let go of the need to know what each day will bring and be with whatever happens in your life.

- Be mindful that life is not always going to be perfect, even when you are really trying. Use this technique as a way to accept the bad things in your life and then let them go without judging yourself or blaming yourself for them.

- Begin to look at your thoughts or feelings as tools or indicators of what is going on inside and outside of yourself, not as things you have control over all the time. Don't try to force them out of your mind.

When you can accept that your thoughts and feelings are not necessarily "good" or "bad," you can learn to accept them without judging them.

Accepting these thoughts and feelings for what they are will help decrease their power over your life. It will give you more freedom, instead of being controlled by every fearful thought or feeling that comes into your mind.

3. The I Am _____ Exercise

This exercise can be used as a tool for self-acceptance and self-forgiveness and can be performed by anyone at any time.

The I Am _______ exercise was created to help you let go of the need to constantly be in control of yourself and your life and accept everything for what it is (including you). It will help you release the need for perfection, perfectionism, and the fear of failure.

How to do this:

Step 1: Make a Statement

Make a statement about yourself (i.e., I am ______), and then respond to the following questions:

Q: How can you be sure of your identity?

A   **:**

____

(You can answer this question honestly by saying things like, "Because I have a body that is my own" or "Because I have a mind that thinks all the time and I can't stop myself from thinking." (It may not be what others think, but it is how you know, and if you don't feel good about it, this exercise may be helpful to you.)

Q: If you knew that you were ______, how would you know?

A   **:**

____

(You can answer this question honestly by saying things like, "Because I feel good" or "Because I feel bad," or "I am not happy with who I am." (Most people can relate to this.)

Q: What would you do if you knew that you were _____?

A   :

____

(You can answer this question honestly by saying things like, "I would feel bad," or "I might try to change myself."

Q: What if you were in a situation where _____?

A   :

____

(You can answer this question honestly by saying things like, "It would feel bad" or "It would feel good," or "It wouldn't be me." (You may be here on Earth to be the best you can be, or to give hope to others who are feeling hopeless. Or you may be here for any other reason that you see fit.)

This step is essential because it allows you to mentally differentiate between who you are and who you believe you are. Once that distinction is made, it should be much easier for you to let go of the need for perfectionism, the need always to know what life is going to be like for you, the need to know where things will lead, and the need for control.

Step 2: The Process of Letting Go

In this step, the process of going is broken down into three steps: accepting and letting go, changing, and knowing. For each of these processes, you will answer 3 questions designed to help you learn how to let go and change. You can do this exercise by yourself or with others.

Step 2.1: Accepting and Letting Go

Q: What does it feel like to accept myself for who I am?

A: ____

Q: How would things change I accepted myself for who I am?

A   **:**

____

(You may think "nothing," but the truth is something always happens when you accept yourself in any situation.)

Q: What does it feel like to stop trying to change myself?

A   **:**

____

(For example, "I am free of all my fears, and I can say things without worrying if they will be taken in the wrong way.")

These questions help you see that all you have to do is accept what you are, and then let go and change. Perfectionism and the fear of failing will disappear once you let go of the need to be perfect.

Step 2.2: Changing

Q: What does it feel like to change my perception of who I am?

A: ____

(For example, "I feel like being this way is not okay with me.")

Q: How would things be different if I changed my perception of who I am?

A   :

____

(You may think "nothing" but the truth is something always happens when we change ourselves in any situation. And if we don't want to accept those changes, it will only cause us more issues in the future.)

Q: What does it feel like to stop trying to control all the thoughts and situations that come my way?

A: ____

Step 2.3: Knowing

Q: What does it feel like to know who I truly am?

A   :

____

(You are probably feeling uncomfortable because you have not been able to see that you are actually good enough. For example, "I have never seen myself as being good enough before, and I have always tried to be better, so I am not sure that I like the way that feels.")

Q: How would things be different if I knew who I truly was?

A :

(For example, "It feels good to know who I am because now I can become the best version of myself.")

Q: What does it feel like to stop trying to be someone I am not?

A :

(For example, "I feel good knowing I am the way I am, so I can stop and enjoy myself. I don't need to keep changing myself in ways that make me feel uncomfortable.")

Step 2 is all about looking within yourself and taking the time to see what it would be like if you did change. Step 2 consists of examining how you view yourself or your self-image, as well as what it would be like if you stopped trying to control or alter yourself. Take the time to see yourself for who you really are and understand that this is okay. With this knowledge, you will be able to let go and change your need for perfectionism, need for control, and fear of failure.

Step 3: Accepting What Is Left

Step 3 is about changing your thoughts and feelings about yourself. Before you can change or let go of who you think you are, it is important first to accept yourself for who you are now.

Step 3 deals with thoughts and feelings. You will learn how to think in ways that allow good things to happen and to feel good about yourself even when everything seems so hard. We change negative beliefs into positive ones by using three methods: changing a belief, facing fear, and moving towards your emotion.

a. Changing a Belief

Sometimes, we have to change the way we think about something. For example, you might have a belief that says that if you are not perfect, you are no good. We will call this a negative belief because it hurts your life. Maybe you have learned that you can't stand not being perfect. Next time you have the urge to be perfect or your fear of failure starts to go off inside of yourself, stop and change the belief by doing this:

- Think about your thought differently, for example: Instead of, "I have to be perfect," think "I don't need to be perfect," or "I am who I am." You are in control of your life, your emotions don't control you. You are perfect enough by simply being yourself and choosing to be nice to yourself and others.

- See if a different thought pops into your head. Maybe you don't need to be perfect, or maybe the thought might be, "I am just trying to please myself and others by doing my best." This way, you can see how damaging your negative thoughts have been.

- You can also do this by watching more TV or turning on a favorite song that always makes you happy. Doing this will allow your mind to go somewhere else where it won't think about being perfect or feeling bad about yourself.

- Telling yourself that you are the one in control of your life will give you the confidence to do better. By changing your negative belief, you can let go of this part of yourself and move on with your life.

b. Facing Fear

When we have a negative thought or feeling about something, we must understand that these thoughts and feelings are not real but just in our heads. They can cause us to be sad or to think in ways that are not good for us. Now is the time to confront your fear or the portion of you that does not want things to change, or that believes you are fine as you are. This is called "facing fear." Once you are able to confront your fear, you can begin to modify your feelings and thoughts about yourself.

How to do it:

- Think about yourself and the fear or issue that is bothering you. You might want to begin with an event from your past, or something that makes you feel bad now. Choose a place where it is easy for your mind to focus and understand what might be causing some of your thoughts or feelings.

- Look at what you are afraid of and figure out why you are afraid of it. What feeling do you have? What thoughts are telling you this fear is real and true? Understanding why you feel bad or uncomfortable will allow you to see your fear for what it is: merely a thought or feeling.

- Think about what it would be like to let go of this part of yourself. For example, what would happen if you could stop trying to be perfect and change who you are? You might say things like, "If I didn't have to worry about being perfect all the time, I would be able to _______________________________." Or you might think, "When I don't have to change, I will be able to _______________________."

- Now that you understand that your fear is simply a thought or feeling in your head and not real in the world, start seeing yourself letting go of being perfect and letting people love who you really are.

- See yourself slowly letting go of your fear and changing who you are in this instance. You might imagine yourself relaxing or smiling with no worries about what others think of you or what you think of yourself.

- Now that you know how to change when these thoughts or feelings come up, face another part of your life that is bothering you and see if there is a way to address these troublesome thoughts and feelings.

c. Moving Towards Your Emotion

Sometimes your thought or feeling may feel so strong that it does not matter how much you try to change it; it just won't leave you alone. The thought or feeling may be about something that happened to you in the past or something that is troubling you now. Instead of trying to rid yourself of your fear by seeing why it's there, you can try moving towards your emotion.

How to do this:

- Think about what emotion you are experiencing and some things you can do to change how you feel. You might say, "When I feel bad, I usually want to be left alone or be with happy people. I can go outside and talk to a friend who doesn't make me feel bad about myself, or I can imagine myself doing something that will make me happy." Or maybe you say, "When I am upset about something, my best way of feeling better is to talk to someone or do something that stirs my emotions."

- Look at where these emotions come from and why you feel the emotion is there. By thinking about what makes you feel bad, you can feel better by looking at how things are now and only thinking about this one thing instead of all the other thoughts or emotions.

- See yourself doing something else to get rid of your negative thoughts or feelings. You might imagine yourself talking to someone or doing another activity, so your mind isn't busy thinking about past events or what someone might say about you.

- Next, move towards the feeling with no distractions and without trying to change anything. See what it feels when your mind doesn't try to get you to feel bad about yourself.

- Whenever you feel upset, see yourself moving closer to the emotion by saying, "When I'm sad, I will feel __________________, etc."

- It may take time to gradually move towards the emotion you are afraid of. But once your mind begins to feel like it wants to move towards your emotion, you will be able to make changes in how you feel and think about yourself.

- Finally, when you are closer to your emotion and you feel like you want to let go of it, try doing so in a few simple ways. Let's say your fear is of being sad, and it feels like the only way to let go of being sad is to get help from someone. You might say something like this: "When I'm feeling sad, I will ______________." Or you could imagine yourself talking about your emotions with someone you trust.

Moving towards your emotion will help you let go of the negative feelings and start moving towards letting go of your fear too.

The I Am ______ technique deals with putting aside a thought or feeling, then slowly seeing yourself changing so your mind stops thinking about it. This technique might not work if your thoughts or feelings demand excessive attention or your feelings are too strong for you. When this happens, don't force yourself to keep trying to let go. But if you think of this as a process that is hard but worth it, it might allow you to feel better about yourself in the long run. The more often you practice this technique, the more comfortable and confident you will become with your mind and emotions.

Accepting feelings, whether bad or good, and not judging yourself for feeling the way you do can help you to be more aware of the way you think and feel. It can also help you be more accepting of yourself as a person. As you begin to understand why you have these thoughts or feelings, you will be able to change how they make you feel, even if they are always with you.

Sometimes seeking external help from a qualified professional is beneficial if you're having trouble coming to terms with negative emotions and thoughts. The type of professional you see may be a trained therapist or social worker, psychologist, psychiatrist, or another mental health provider.

In the past, doctors often treated emotions or mental problems as illnesses in their own right and prescribed medications to help overcome their symptoms. This is no longer the case in most countries that have adopted modern treatments for mental illnesses. It is important to consider whether your negative emotions are a sign that you need help from a professional.

If you have been dealing with an emotional issue for a long time and don't feel better after trying various self-help methods, assistance from a professional may be helpful.

If you are unsure of the kind of assistance you require, speak with a friend or relative who will understand your thoughts and feelings. Alternatively, some professionals have been trained in the art of reading minds and emotions, so strike up a conversation with them and see what happens.

A professional can help you if your emotions or negative thoughts are interfering with your daily life. These thoughts and feelings are fine when occasional, but it is a problem if they begin to control your life. If you feel like this is happening, professional help might be able to give you tools to change your negative thinking into less emotional thought patterns. This can make it easier for you to think more positively.

PART 3 - WHEN SHOULD NEGATIVE EMOTIONS NOT BE CONTROLLED?

P art 3

When Should Negative Emotions Not Be Controlled?

CHAPTER 7: WHEN SHOULD NEGATIVE EMOTIONS NOT BE CONTROLLED?

A crucial component of overall health is emotional well-being. Emotionally balanced people have control over their thoughts, feelings, and actions. They can handle the difficulties of life. They can remain optimistic and recover from setbacks. They have positive self-esteem and satisfying relationships.

Being emotionally stable does not necessarily entail constant joy. It suggests that you are aware of your emotions. You can control them no matter what happens. Emotionally healthy people still feel stress, rage, and sadness. But they are skilled at controlling their negative emotions. They can recognize when a problem is too much for them to handle alone. Additionally, they are aware of when to consult a doctor and when to turn to friends and family for support.

There are times when intense emotions should not be controlled. If you have just lost a loved one, it would be unwise to remain in complete control of your thoughts and feelings. Grief is a typical response to a death, a loss, and other major events. A period of mourning and grieving is necessary to begin the healing process. Similarly, if you are under physical attack or your life is in danger, it is impossible to remain calm and rational. The proper response is immediate self-defense or escape. You cannot afford to worry about negative consequences when more pressing matters are at hand, such as staying alive or protecting yourself from harm.

Impacts of Constantly Experiencing Negative Emotions

If you are constantly repressing your emotions and not dealing with them, then they will continue to manifest in other ways throughout your life. Some of these include:

Toxic Relationships with Loved ones and Work Colleagues

Constantly suppressing your emotions can lead to feeling distant from loved ones and coworkers. Externally, it may appear as though you have everything under control, but internally, you have been dealing with a great deal of stress. Holding on to these feelings may feel good for a short time, but it will eventually weigh down your body and make you feel exhausted. If this happens more than once or twice, the people around you may notice that something is not quite right for you; however, if this is a repeat pattern, they may grow frustrated or upset with your behavior. They may feel as though there is something wrong but not understand what is happening, and it can be difficult for them to communicate this to you if they do not understand it themselves. This can cause a rift in your relationship because it is hard for them to understand why you are upset or why you seem distant.

Several factors make dealing with your emotions more difficult and may even cause you to isolate yourself from people that love you. Besides how often your emotions are repressed and how much stress you are dealing with, there is also the story that your mind tells about what is happening to you. If you believe that everything bad in life is your fault, then it can feel as though it is; this may cause you to isolate yourself even further because of the guilt that comes with the belief. When there is a lot of stress in your life, this may seem like an explanation for why negative feelings occur. This can easily lead to severe isolation, which can be difficult to overcome. It can also lead to feeling like you have no control over your life, which serves to strengthen your belief that you cannot deal with your emotions and the pain they bring.

Lack of Growth and Improvement in Your Life

If you constantly repress your emotions, it will be very hard to improve your life or grow as a person. Repressing negative emotions causes stress on your body, eventually leading to health issues and a lower quality of life. The less healthy you feel, the harder it is to move forward with anything because it makes you feel stuck and unable to do more than get by from day to day. When this occurs repeatedly, it becomes easier for the mind to accept that nothing can be done to change the situation or alleviate the negative emotions or stress. If this happens, you may seem to be living your life just fine on the outside, making it hard for loved ones and close friends to see that you are struggling. But you do not have the energy to move forward, and the less energy you have, the less likely you are to be able to improve and make your life better.

The more negative emotions you experience, the more stress you will feel, and the less time you will have to deal with anything else. You may also feel like your life is a nightmare because things seem to be going wrong at all times, which can make it difficult to focus on what is good in your life. People around you may not understand why the situation seems so bad for you and why you feel as though nothing can be done about your situation. This may cause them to feel frustrated, which can strain your relationship with them and eventually cause you to feel isolated from people you care about.

Loneliness and Feelings of Being Lost

If you are constantly repressing your emotions, you will probably feel lost because it means you lack support. You may not want to reach out and talk about what is going on with people because you believe this may make things worse. As a result, the emotions become worse than ever before. If this occurs, it may be challenging for you to lead a healthy lifestyle because you will be preoccupied with worry all the time. It may feel like your heart has been ripped out of you, making it difficult for you to feel any joy or happiness. You may wonder why life has become such a nightmare, and you may struggled to get through each day.

Other people may feel there is no reason to talk to you when you feel so down, while they are happier than ever. If you do not feel like you can talk to anyone else and that no one understands what is going on, it can be easy to fall into a deep depression and withdraw from the people around you.

Alcohol Abuse or Drug Addiction

Repressing your emotions can make it very difficult for your mind to snap out of the stuck state, leading to an almost constant feeling of anxiety and stress. This may lead you to develop an addiction to cope with the emotions you are repressing. You may begin to abuse alcohol or drugs because they give you a way to feel better. This can cause your life to go completely off the rails.

If you continue to drink or abuse drugs, it can lead to a complete loss of control. The more hopeless you feel, the more likely you will be to fall into addiction because it will seem like there is no way out of the situation, and everything will feel like it is going wrong. This can make it very difficult to realize that the problem is with your mind and not the way things actually are in your life.

An Overall Lack of Happiness

Happiness comes from feeling healthy, meeting your needs, and getting through the day without feeling stressed or anxious. If you cannot meet these basic needs and have a lot of repressed feelings, then it makes sense that there will be a loss of joy in your life.

If you are constantly suppressing your emotions and cannot healthily deal with them, then it may be a struggle to get through the day and correct the problems in your life.

Self-Destruction

If you are always repressing your emotions, it is likely that you will be doing things to hurt yourself or others instead of dealing with your feelings. You may also become more concerned about the safety and well-being of others rather than your own.

If you have repressed your emotions for so long, it will likely lead to a complete loss of self-control and the inability to help yourself or others in any way.

A Lack of Care for Others

If you are repressing your emotions, it may cause you to not care as much about the people around you. People will not be able to rely on you if they do not know what is happening with you. This can make it very difficult for your relationships to work and lead you to feel isolated. If you cannot think about others, you will be less likely to develop friendships and relationships that help your mental health.

The Feeling that You Have Lost Yourself

Constantly repressing your emotions can make it difficult for you to feel like you have a real sense of self. This can cause some people to want to die since they are not being honest with themselves or others.

If you keep repressing your emotions, it can make it more difficult to feel like you have any sense of reality. This means that it will also be increasingly difficult for you to feel like yourself, which may lead to depression and anxiety. This will make it harder for people to understand and relate to who you are and will likely cause your mental state to worsen.

These are just some of the problems that people can experience if they constantly repress their emotions. Repressing your emotions makes it very difficult to live a healthy and happy life. If you feel any of the above is happening to you, you should start working on overcoming your emotional issues so that things can begin to work out for you in the future. The more you choose not to put yourself first, the more these problems will likely cause you stress and anxiety and make it difficult for you to do simple day-to-day tasks.

Common Health Issues

The following are some of the most common negative health issues brought on by repressing emotions:

Obesity

Repressing your emotions can have an enormous impact on your ability to lose weight. If you have a lot of stress in your life, you may develop an eating disorder because you believe eating is the only thing that can help relieve the stress. This can be a slippery slope, as people who are constantly depressed and experiencing overwhelming negative emotions may find it easier to overeat.

Women are 50 percent more likely than men to develop an eating disorder when depressed, according to the American Psychological Association. However, this does not preclude men from developing eating disorders. This is so prevalent because of how individuals perceive food and how they feel once they begin eating. If you have any self-esteem issues, it can make it easier to give in to emotional eating.

Many people end up using food as a coping mechanism rather than a source of nutrition. Repressed feelings can make it much more likely for you to begin using food as a source of happiness rather than something that is going to help your body.

High Blood Pressure

When someone has repressed their emotions for a long period, they will likely be dealing with a lot of anxiety about things in their life. This can cause them to become anxious, which may lead them down a path where they develop high blood pressure.

High blood pressure is the heart pumping much more blood than it should. This is a very serious condition that can lead to several health problems and death. If you are repressing your emotions, you may be having trouble controlling your stress and anxiety levels. This means that it will be easy for you to develop high blood pressure because you will have more stress than ever before, and your body will be trying to keep up with this by pumping out more blood.

People with repressed emotions may develop chronic high blood pressure when they deal with these feelings over a long period. This is why it is very important to learn to control your emotions. If you do not, your blood pressure can start to rise, and you may feel like the walls are closing in around you.

Hypertension can lead to a number of health problems, according to the Mayo Clinic. It must be addressed immediately because, if left untreated, it can lead to conditions such as coronary heart disease, heart attack, stroke, and even death.

Sleep Apnea

If you have developed high blood pressure and other problems related to repressing your emotions, it is much more likely that you will also start developing sleep apnea. When you stop breathing during the night, it can be impossible for you to get a full night's rest.

Sleep apnea is something that most people never really think about until it ends up causing them to feel tired or have trouble sleeping. People who have repressed their emotions are very likely to end up going through these issues. Eventually, sleep apnea will make it impossible for them to rest, which will cause much more stress and make it harder for them to enjoy life.

According to the American Academy of Sleep Medicine, people with sleep apnea are at a much higher risk of many other health issues. When they cannot get a full night's rest, they will suffer from fatigue and be unable to function normally throughout the day. This can be very frustrating for people with sleep apnea because they will not be able to enjoy life the way that most people do because their bodies will not be able to function properly.

Skin Issues

People who have constant repressed emotions often experience issues with their skin. When you are trying to repress your emotions, your body will react out of sheer exhaustion. You will have issues with your skin because your body is not getting the nutrients it needs to take care of itself.

Skin problems that you might experience include rashes and outbreaks; dry, itchy skin; and more. This is because it is very difficult for you to deal with any stressors in your life, which will lead you to keep holding onto these emotions for days on end. Suppose you do not let out these emotions regularly. In that case, they will build up and cause you to start developing rashes and other skin problems that will not be easy for you to get over.

According to the Mayo Clinic, skin problems can affect anyone. Still, they tend to affect people who have repressed their emotions for a long time. Because your body isn't able to get rid of the toxins that are slowly accumulating when your emotions are held in for a long time, it is likely that you will start experiencing severe skin problems.

Lowered Immune System

The act of repressing your emotions can have a very serious impact on your immune system as well. When you are constantly holding on to these emotions, your immune system will go into overdrive trying to deal with the pain. This can lead you to develop an array of health problems and cause serious side effects, such as a loss of energy and a lack of focus on things that are truly important to you.

If you are trying to repress your emotions, it is very difficult for your body to get rid of all of the toxins that are present within it at any given time. They will continue building up, causing your immune system to not work as well as it should.

Frequent Anxiety and Panic Attacks

People constantly holding on to their emotions are very likely to develop anxiety and panic attacks because they will not be able to deal with the challenges of life. According to the American Psychological Association, people who have emotional issues such as anxiety and panic attacks are more likely to make poor decisions in their day-to-day lives. You won't likely be very happy in life if you're constantly attempting to suppress these feelings, and your actions are probably not going to be all that constructive.

You may end up developing a number of serious health problems if you struggle with repressing your emotions. However, you can learn how to deal with your emotions positively and eliminate these issues. You can do exercises to help you deal with these emotions rather than trying to repress them. It might take some time to develop coping mechanisms, but in the long run, it will be much more advantageous.

Life is complex. Ignoring part of the emotional spectrum we experience while living that complex life can reduce our level of contentment and lead to a shorter life span.

The Path to Improved Health

According to research, emotional stability is a skill. You can make changes to become happier and more emotionally healthy. Here's how:

1. Evaluate Your Current Emotional State

The first step is to evaluate your current emotional state. Identification is key. If you know why you are sad or angry, you can take steps to prevent the problems from happening again. You will be more likely to respond as needed if you know what caused your emotions in the first place.

2. Embrace Your Feelings

Negative emotions can be healthy at certain times. They can be a powerful reminder to take care of ourselves and others. You should not ignore or suppress them. Your feelings will only get worse if you ignore them. Suppressing your feelings will only lead to them popping out when you least expect them. To effectively control your emotions, first notice what you are feeling, then accept your feelings as natural responses to the world around you, and finally direct those feelings in a useful way that can benefit yourself or others.

3. Embrace Your Thoughts

You can alter your thoughts to alter how you feel. The more you focus on positive thoughts, the more positive feelings you will experience. Focusing on positive thoughts and feelings can also help you realize when you are in danger of making a negative situation worse. Once you become aware that negative emotions are present, it is easier to recognize them and respond effectively to them before they develop into something worse. You can then work to correct or escape the situation as necessary. Similarly, if you frequently think negative thoughts, they will make a poor impression on those around you. It is easier to have a healthy opinion of yourself when your mental processes are functioning at their best.

4. Develop Healthy Habits

By developing healthy habits, you will be less likely to experience negative feelings in the future. These habits include:

a. Eating a balanced diet

A healthy diet consists of various fruits, vegetables, and grains. If your diet lacks certain nutrients and contains too many unhealthy additives, it can cause feelings of sadness or anxiety.

Foods that are good for your mental health:

1. Nuts and seeds: walnuts, hemp seeds, hazelnuts, almonds

Omega-3 fatty acids, an essential fatty acid, are abundant in nuts and seeds (EFA). The body requires Omega-3 EFA as building blocks for other fats and proteins. They also have been shown to promote healthy brain function and improve mood. This is one of the main reasons why so many people use nut and seed butters on their toast or salads. They are especially beneficial for those who experience low mood and anxiety. The best way to incorporate more seeds and nuts into your diet is by adding them to smoothies.

Vitamin E, which serves a variety of purposes in the body, is also abundant in nuts and seeds. Vitamin E promotes healthy cell membranes and may play an important role in preventing cancer and heart disease. Vitamin E also plays a vital role in manufacturing red blood cells, constructing DNA molecules, maintaining healthy skin and hair, maintaining immune function, and more. Finally, vitamin E assists in fighting free radicals that can damage cells and cause diseases such as cancer by enabling cellular repair. This helps our mental health by reducing the oxidation of fatty acids in the brain and can result in a better mood.

2. Vegetables: leafy greens, broccoli, and cauliflower

Leafy green vegetables are rich in vitamin B6 and folate (folic acid), which are essential for healthy brain function. They also contain additional nutrients that are good for the nervous system, like iron and magnesium. Another great benefit of leafy greens is that they are high in antioxidants, which help fight the aging process and promote cellular repair. These factors could potentially improve mental health by reducing oxidative damage that would otherwise contribute to neurodegenerative disorders such as dementia or Alzheimer's.

Calcium is abundant in leafy greens, which supports a healthy nervous system. Calcium is an essential mineral that can help to prevent and fight depression by promoting the production of serotonin and other neurotransmitters in our bodies. Broccoli, cauliflower, and other cruciferous vegetables provide us with isothiocyanates, which may protect us against certain cancers. Our memory, learning capabilities, and general cognition tend to decline as we age. We will be less likely to suffer from issues related to mental health as we age if we can maintain a healthy brain through a diet rich in leafy greens.

3. Fruits: pears, apples, and berries

Fructose, which is good for mental health, can be found in fruits. Fructose is an essential component of the body's carbohydrate metabolism system. It plays a key role in the conversion of liver glycogen into glucose and helps to maintain proper brain levels of glucose. A healthy nervous system increases blood flow to the brain, and healthy brain function is all supported by fruits' abundance of vitamins, minerals, and potassium.

Fruits vary in their levels of healthfulness. Anthocyanins, a type of phytonutrient found in berries like blueberries and blackberries, are highly concentrated in berries. These red pigments are thought to have a variety of health advantages, including enhancing mental health by shielding the brain from free radical-induced oxidative damage. Anthocyanins also help reduce inflammation in the body, including in the brain, which is important for modulating mood and preventing depression. Other good choices include citrus fruits such as pomegranate (which contains phytochemicals that can boost the antioxidant activity of vitamin C) and berries like strawberries or raspberries (which contain phenolic acid) pomegranates, which are rich in omega-3 fatty acids.

All fruits are good choices, but some are more beneficial than others. Fruits that contain a decent amount of fructose and vitamin C tend to be more beneficial than fruits that do not. Fruits that contain a lot of anthocyanins (e.g., blueberries) are also much better choices than other fruits (e.g., kiwis and cantaloupes).

4. Grains: quinoa and brown rice

The more grains you eat, the better. They are a good source of carbohydrates, essential for keeping our blood sugar levels stable and regulating our moods. This can prevent issues such as bipolar disorder and depression. Other grains that are beneficial to mental health include quinoa and teff, which have higher levels of protein than most other grains and contain all nine essential amino acids (building blocks of protein) that our bodies can't produce. These are the building blocks of neurotransmitters in our brain and are essential for producing new neurons – thus, our neurons are constantly growing.

Additionally, grains contain a lot of B-complex vitamins, which help keep the brain and nervous system healthy and thus support normal nervous system function. B-complex vitamins' main benefits are that they promote a healthy nervous system and help ward off depression. Quinoa and teff are especially good choices because they contain all B vitamins without the added calories that other grains have.

5. Dairy products: eggs and yogurt

Dairy products are rich in protein, which is essential for healthy brain function. Protein is used to create and maintain new brain cells, including neurons and glial cells. The presence of calcium, vitamins and other essential nutrients that help to maintain a healthy nervous system further contributes to their beneficial effects on mental health.

Milk, yogurt, and cheese are particularly beneficial because they contain high levels of protein and calcium. Calcium is an essential mineral that works together with other vital nutrients like vitamin D to promote healthy nervous system function. Several studies have linked healthy calcium levels with a lower risk of depression. Although there is evidence that milk may increase the risk of developing some cancers, its benefits far outweigh its risks. Egg yolks are also beneficial, but they do contribute more cholesterol and saturated fat than milk or yogurt.

6. Fish and beans: tuna, sardines, salmon, white beans, and other seafood

The association between fish consumption and mental health has been well documented. Fish is an essential component of our diet since it provides vitamins, minerals, and low-fat proteins that our bodies cannot manufacture. Although we don't yet know why fish consumption is linked to better mental health, it is reasonable to assume that these vitamins and minerals are one of the reasons. Fish also contains omega-3 fatty acids, which have anti-inflammatory effects on the body. These are important for overall health, but they have a profound effect on brain function as well because they promote healthy nerve cell growth in the brain by helping to maintain a balanced immune response.

Fish is versatile, and it can be prepared in a variety of ways. Sardines are the best choice because they contain less mercury than other types of fish; salmon and tuna are also good choices, especially if they are wild-caught. White beans are also good options, as they are rich in fiber-rich B vitamins and contain all essential amino acids. Beans are high in phytoestrogens (very weakly estrogenic compounds), which may help lower estrogen levels and improve mood while promoting bone and heart health.

7. Herbs and spices: cinnamon, turmeric, sage, black pepper, clove

Herbs and spices do not contain any calories or fat; they are very high in phytochemicals that promote overall health by preventing inflammation in the body. A growing number of studies suggest that dietary inflammation may play a role in the prevention of depression and that inflammatory foods may exacerbate symptoms of depression by elevating levels of inflammatory markers in the body's tissues. According to some studies, those who eat more spices typically experience depression at lower rates than those who do not. Herbs and spices that can be beneficial include sage, cinnamon, cloves, and turmeric.

Developing healthy eating habits and choosing the right foods for healthy brain function is an excellent way to prevent depression, improve mood, and prevent the onset of numerous chronic diseases.

b. Exercise

Regular exercise can help promote mental health in several ways:

- It provides mental and physical stimulation for the body, increasing neurotransmitter levels and neurotransmitter foundations in the brain.

- It is useful for clearing the mind and giving people an opportunity to reflect on their day.

- It helps prevent anxiety by promoting a feeling of relaxation.

- It can be rewarding because many people derive a sense of accomplishment from working out.

Sports or exercise programs that are interactive are also beneficial because people can build social skills and relationships that aid mental health.

It is recommended that people have approximately 30 minutes of moderate physical activity every day. This is typically accomplished through cardio exercises like jogging, biking, or swimming. However, more intense bursts of activity such as weight training are also beneficial. They help to boost energy and promote mood by increasing the release of neurotransmitters. Maintaining a healthy sleep schedule is also crucial for enhancing mental health because it enables the brain to work all day effectively without getting tired. Lastly, maintaining healthy body weight is important because it helps reduce stress levels and maintain a healthy mood.

The benefits of exercise are numerous. Regular exercise can alleviate anxiety, improve mood and prevent the onset of depression.

c. Getting plenty of sleep

Sleeping allows the body to rejuvenate, rebalance and recharge. It also allows the brain to process information, synthesize memories and form new neural connections. While a person is asleep, several neurochemical processes occur that are important for overall health and well-being. For example, while asleep, the body produces powerful antioxidants called glutathione that help to protect the nervous system against damage. Getting good sleep makes it easier to maintain a healthy weight because the blood sugar levels are kept at a constant level.

Individual needs for sleep vary, but for optimal performance and general health, most people require between 7-9 hours each night. Obesity, overmedication, and self-destructive behaviors are all linked to sleep durations of less than six hours. Lack of sleep is associated with decreased stress tolerance, depression, and fatigue.

For those who do not get enough sleep regularly, there are several ways to improve the quality of sleep without increasing the amount of time spent sleeping:

- **Proper timing:** Try to sleep and wake up at the same time every day, even on weekends.

- **Wind-down routine:** Prepare for bed by turning off all electronics such as TVs, tablets, cell phones, and computers.

- **Prioritizing rest:** Don't worry if a situation arises that might prevent you from getting enough sleep; your health is more important than things like work deadlines and networking occasions.

- **Eating habits:** Avoid eating any heavy meals within 2

hours of bedtime because it prevents the digestive system from working properly, thus preventing a person from getting into a deep sleep state. (Deep sleep occurs in cycles of 90 minutes.)

- **Exercise:** Exercising too late at night can make it difficult to get to sleep.

- **Sleep routine:** Create an environment that is suited for rest, such as dimming the lights, turning off any electronics, and trying relaxation techniques like meditation or deep breathing.

- **Bedroom environment:** To increase your likelihood of falling asleep at a reasonable hour, make your bedroom dark, quiet, and comfortable. You can also help yourself establish a healthy sleeping pattern by adjusting the bedroom's temperature.

- **Avoid caffeine:** Caffeine is a stimulant; before bedtime, it can keep someone up and prevent them from getting a good night's sleep.

- **Regularity:** If a person constantly misses sleep, they will develop a deep sleep deficit, which means that the body is lacking adequate amounts of oxygen and nutrients. This prevents an individual from feeling well-rested and may cause symptoms of depression.

Sleep issues can occur for various reasons, most commonly due to stress or anxiety. People may encounter common issues, including insomnia, restless sleep, and nightmares. Nightmares are caused by a combination of hormones and brain chemistry; however, they do not necessarily indicate any underlying psychological issues. The best way to deal with sleep issues is to seek the help of a professional. However, several techniques are useful in the short term.

d. Not smoking

Smoking is harmful for a number of reasons, including the fact that it raises the body's levels of the stress hormone adrenaline, which can result in elevated stress and cravings for junk food. If a person is addicted to nicotine but does not currently smoke, they will still benefit from avoiding second-hand smoke.

e. Refraining from alcohol abuse

Excessive alcohol intake can produce feelings of relaxation and reduce stress; however, it strains the heart and liver and causes damage to vital organs such as the brain, nervous system, and gastrointestinal tract. Alcohol abuse is associated with social dependence, depression, and anxiety disorders due to the inability to function without drinking or having immense anxiety when attempting sobriety.

f. Making time for hobbies and social connections

People who are involved in rewarding activities outside of work feel less stressed, have heightened levels of energy, are more effective at achieving their daily goals, and as a result, sleep better. Conversely, people who do not take pleasure in life may become depressed and anxious.

5. Deal With Your Environment

The environment will affect your emotions, and as such, your sleep. If you are consistently experiencing negative emotions, it is a good idea to look at what is going on in your life. For example, if you are just not feeling well, it might be wise for you to visit the doctor. If something about your environment is making you feel worse, try moving out of that environment. If you are living in a home that is too hot, is full of noise, or dirty, try to find another home to live in. You can also ask your landlord to do something about the situation.

6. Get Therapy

Therapy is a great way to start feeling better. There are many different types of therapy that you can try out. You should try out various forms until you find the one that best suits your needs because everyone will react to therapy differently. Cognitive behavioral therapy, relationship counseling, and marriage counseling are a few of the more popular forms of therapy that people use.

In general, therapy is a safe and effective way of getting relief from illness and stress. However, therapy does not work for everyone because it is a very personal form of treatment. If you hate how the therapist talks to you or looks at you, then it is most likely not the right therapist for you. Most therapists have the best interest of their clients at heart, and you will eventually find the right therapist, so don't give up.

Managing negative emotions is essential for mental and physical health. Happiness is a good thing, but it doesn't mean ignoring or suppressing all the feelings that flow through your system – acknowledging these feelings plays a vital role in maintaining health.

CHAPTER 8: EXPRESSING EMOTIONS SAFELY

Emotions are crucial to life. Numerous aspects of daily life are fraught with intense emotion. Emotions may cause us to change our actions and outlook in many ways. However, emotions are not something to be taken lightly. They can cause us to act in harmful ways or perceive things that may be untrue about ourselves and others. Emotions can cause us to hurt other people, put ourselves in harm's way or hurt our self-esteem. It is important for us to learn how to express our emotions safely and appropriately.

For many people, emotions remain mysterious, confusing, and difficult to express constructively. Many people have trouble expressing their emotions and feelings because they don't know how to communicate or want to avoid conflict with others. People who haven't learned how to properly express their emotions frequently believe that others don't care about them and that their emotions are too big for them to handle. It is important for us to learn how to express our emotions safely so that we can foster healthy relationships.

Benefits of Expressing Emotions Safely

1. It helps us better handle the world around us.

When you can express emotions safely, you can better handle any situation that comes your way. When you can understand and deal with your emotions appropriately and healthily, you can make better decisions because raging emotions do not cloud you. When you cannot express your feelings safely, your feelings may cause you to react inappropriately. The inappropriate reactions might cause you to say or do something dangerous or hurtful. It might also cause you harm as well as the people around you.

The ability to express your emotions, whether they are positive or negative, is crucial for both your physical and mental well-being. Healthily expressing emotions can help you to have clearer thinking and better decision-making skills.

2. Your moods will be more stable

You will be less likely to feel angry or depressed when you can express your emotions healthily. You will also be less likely to feel anxious or scared. It is much easier to remain positive when we can express our emotions properly. When you are not able to express your true emotions, it is much more difficult for people to know how you feel about something because they may not be able to read your facial expressions and body language. When you can express yourself better, it is more likely that you will be able to come to a resolution about your feelings in a manner that is beneficial for everyone involved.

3. It enhances your relationships with others.

A healthy relationship with another person can have many benefits. When you can express your emotions properly, then you will be able to have an open and honest conversation with the person who is closest to you. When you can talk about your feelings with a partner, you will also have an easier time understanding what they are feeling. Having a better understanding of one another will make it easier for you to resolve any potential problems.

When you can express your emotions properly, you will have a much easier time understanding what is going on with other people. You will be able to understand how other people feel and why they do the things they do, as well as how you should respond when those situations arise.

4. It cultivates positive self-esteem.

Being open about your emotions and understanding how you really feel makes you feel more confident in yourself. Often people feel like they need to pretend like they are feeling better than they do to avoid conflict, anger, or disappointment in others. But when you have a positive self-image, then you are capable of accepting the way that things are without feeling the need to hide behind a mask.

5. It helps to heal from past traumas.

Many people have lived through difficult times in their lives and will often carry those negative emotions around with them. They do not know how to express their emotions or why they are feeling the way that they are. They may not even be certain about how to express their true emotions. When you need help taming those negative emotions, expressing your feelings can be very effective for your recovery process.

People who have experienced some trauma in the past may find that they are unable to express their emotions safely. They may believe that they have done something wrong and that others will be angry with them if they express those negative emotions. This can lead to a lot of anxiety that can prevent these people from talking about the incident and leaving it buried in the past. It may cause them to avoid thinking about what happened. When these emotions recur at random times, they can become intense enough to interfere with their daily lives and physical health. People who have experienced trauma will often be less likely to leave dangerous situations because they have a hard time trusting others. People who feel as if they have been victimized may also find it very difficult to be intimate or trust anyone.

Without the ability to express their emotions, people might not be able to fully recover from their past traumas. These are often things the mind will block out, making it very hard for those memories to resurface. When you can express your emotions, it can help make some of those memories more accessible so you can deal with them in a more healthy way and move on with your life.

Expressing our emotions is like giving feedback on how we feel about ourselves and those around us. We need to be able to speak up about our feelings for others and ourselves. Often we do not express these feelings because we are afraid of what people will think about us. This can cause problems in both our relationships and our mental health. It is important to know that there are going to be ups and downs with your expression of emotions. Sometimes it can feel good; other times, it can feel terrible. That is normal, but what matters most is how you handle the situation while the emotion is happening.

Tips on Expressing Your Emotions in a Healthy Way

The following will give you some tips on how to express your emotions healthily.

1. Use Verbal Communication

When trying to express your emotions, you must use verbal communication. This can be hard to practice because many of us have grown up not speaking our minds and trying to keep the peace at all times. This can make you feel it is not safe to say what is on your mind, particularly when you are upset. However, it would help if you let the other person know how you feel verbally so that they can understand how you feel. When people do not know how we feel, they cannot help us.

How to do this:

When you are upset with the other person, you must sit down with them and express how you feel. Talk to them about why you are upset and tell them what it is about their actions that made you feel that way. Be honest about your feelings but be sure to listen to what they have to say. If they disagree with your feelings or think that you are overreacting, let them explain their points so you can understand where they are coming from. If possible, try and work out a compromise instead of telling them that they have done or said something wrong. However, if they have done something that hurt your feelings, it is important to tell them so they know how you feel about it.

Being honest about your feelings is important because it is not fair for the other person to find out about the situation through others instead of you. Even if you have worked things out, it is still a good idea to let people know how you feel in case something like this occurs again. It will also give the other person a chance to apologize and make it up to you somehow. Sometimes, they do not know why you are upset or how they can help. This is their opportunity to do so, so they can avoid doing anything else that might upset you in the future.

2. Practice Before You Express Your Emotions

This will not only help you to get a better understanding of your feelings, but it will also help you become more comfortable expressing them. When you are angry or upset about something, it can be hard to put that into words. Practice talking about how you feel about a certain until it becomes easier for you.

How to do this:

Step 1: Write down all the things that are bothering you.

Make a list of all the things you want and need to say, but also include things you want to avoid saying. You can release your feelings and thoughts simply by writing them down. As it can be difficult to speak what we have been thinking, this will be a great chance for you to practice getting those thoughts out of your head and onto the page.

Step 2: Start talking out loud.

Get a good friend or family member and talk out loud to them about how you feel.

Step 3: Keep practicing until it becomes easier for you.

Even though it might not feel like you are ready, keep practicing until it becomes easier for you to express your feelings verbally. Practice makes perfect.

Practicing before you talk to someone can help you to be better prepared in case you become upset or have questions during your conversation. Additionally, it can give you some time to consider the best way to phrase things while still being true to how you are feeling.

3. Nurture Yourself with Positive Affirmations

Positive affirmations teach you to speak to yourself positively. It allows you to realize the good things about yourself and the world around you. This is a fantastic way to boost your self-esteem and feel more at ease with who you are and your life's circumstances. Positive affirmations act as positive reinforcement and help you to feel happy from within.

How to do this:

Step 1: Make a list of positive things about yourself.

You love many things about yourself and the world around you. Start a list of these wonderful things so that you can remember them when you are feeling down in the future.

Some examples of positive affirmations:

- "I have a lot to be thankful for."

- "I have a good attitude about life."

- "I try to be kind to everyone, no matter what they do or say to me."

- "The world is filled with beautiful things, and I try to find them all every day."

- "There is nothing that I could not do if I put my mind to it."

- "I am a good person and always try my best to make others happy."

- "I am strong."

You can also write your own by asking yourself what helps you to feel better about yourself and what makes you happy.

Step 2: Repeat those positive statements while looking into the mirror every day.

Repeat these statements until they start to feel natural. When your brain gets used to hearing them, it will know how to react when something negative comes up. Positive affirmations help you to feel better about yourself so that you can be more confident when you are around other people.

Step 3: Repeat those positive statements whenever you need them.

Make a list of things that make you feel good and hold onto it in an emergency. Positive affirmations give your mind something happy to think about when something negative happens, stopping you from focusing on the bad things around you.

Try and come up with some ways to use positive affirmations to help yourself grow as a person and learn how to express your emotions healthily.

4. Learn How to Say "No."

This is an important step for anyone learning how to express emotions healthily. Learning to say no is a way to take care of yourself by avoiding taking on too much responsibility or doing something that you do not want to be doing. Sometimes, people will say "yes" when they really want to say "no" because they are afraid of being rejected, or because they do not want to hurt anyone. This does not consider your own feelings or what you want from the situation. Sometimes, we have to give in to others, but you must say no when you do not want to do something.

This is a good way of learning to express your emotions healthily. You will also learn how to manage your time better, save money, and save time that could have been spent doing something more productive or enjoyable.

Situations where you can say no include:

1. You feel exhausted or overworked and need some time to yourself.

Say no when feeling this way because it is hard to have fun or enjoy yourself when you know that you have too much work and not enough time to finish it all. Learn how to prioritize your responsibilities so you do not get overworked like this again in the future, but in the meantime, take a break!

2. You are being pressured to buy something that you do not need or want.

Turn it down if you do not want it. Chances are, you will not be able to sell it when you are done with it, so use the money for something else you enjoy instead of a new item that does not match your current wants and needs.

3. You have more responsibilities than usual at home or school and want to take a break from them for a short time to handle other things.

Dealing with obligations by prioritizing them, so they do not get too overwhelming. Learn how to say no, and you will also learn to be more positive toward yourself and others.

4. You are not interested in doing it.

If someone asks you to do something you do not want to do, say no. Some people might think you are being rude, but if the situation does not interest you, why should you do it? Learn to say no and be happy with your decision instead of feeling guilty or obligated to do something you are not interested in.

How do I learn how to say "no"?

- Consider carefully what they are asking of you and what your current obligations are.

- Think about how you feel about the situation and whether or not it is something that you want to do. Sometimes, when people get a request, it is hard for them to say no because they are afraid of what the other person will think of them. Before doing anything, be honest with yourself and ask: "How will I feel if I say 'yes'?"

- Make sure you are not under pressure from anyone else because if there is any pressure involved, you may find yourself saying yes. Say no when you want to because it is your feelings and emotions at stake, not anyone else's.

- If you are still feeling uncomfortable or uncertain about the situation and the responsibilities in front of you, try saying "maybe" instead of "no." This is a way to tell someone that you are thinking about their offer, but you do not want to commit to it just yet. This gives you time to think about it without making any rash decisions and hurting anyone's feelings.

- If all of the above fails, consider taking some time for yourself away from people who are asking too much of you. This is a good way of discovering whether they care about your feelings and your needs or if they think they have a right to take advantage of your time, energy, and emotions. These things should be viewed as your property and not something that others can use or manipulate just because they feel like it.

Saying no is a good way of learning to express yourself and allow yourself to keep everything important to you, such as your time and emotions.

5. Change What You Can

Learning healthy emotional expression is crucial because there are times when we must make the difficult decision to move on from a situation if it cannot be changed or fixed. Sometimes this is the best way to maintain your sanity and stay true to yourself and your beliefs. This implies that there are some situations where we are unable to change or improve things, but it does not imply that you should stop trying to do so.

6. Keep a Journal

This is a simple, easy way to keep track of the things going on in your life and add something positive to it daily. It helps you learn how to express emotions healthily, and helps you notice and record important aspects or takeaways from each day so that no details get lost or forgotten. It is a great way to express yourself and keep your feelings in check. This can also help you notice those feelings that come and go, but that you might not have noticed otherwise.

You can write about your day's experiences, how you felt about something that happened, or what made an impression on you. You can also write about the people who mean a lot to you and why they do. This helps with expression because it gives you a platform for getting out whatever it is that is bothering, obsessing, or occupying your thoughts so that they do not cause problems in other aspects of your life.

7. Nurture Yourself

Be sure not to abandon yourself or neglect your needs. Find that extra bit of love for yourself that allows you to seek out the things that make you happy.

Tips for Nurturing Oneself

a. Listen to music, read a good book, or write in your journal.

This can help you express emotions healthily because it takes you away from whatever is bothering you or getting on your nerves.

b. Take a walk outside, meditate, or watch the clouds go by.

All these things will bring calm to your heart and help you see the beauty in a day.

c. Take care of yourself.

Eat healthy foods and drink water. When you take care of yourself, it will not only make your body stronger and healthier, it will also give you the impression that everything is under control. As long as you are taking care of yourself, you have a strong foundation and can get things done for yourself and others.

d. Do something for someone else.

Volunteer. This is a way to give back to the world and show yourself that you are not alone and that you can help others who might be going through similar situations as yourself. This gives you the chance to resolve any issues with anger, resentment, stress, or anything else you might be experiencing.

When someone is in need of a human connection, you can also help them by simply listening to them or holding their hand.

e. Talk to a friend or family member about what is going on in your life.

This is a great way to help yourself express your emotions healthily and work out what you can do to improve any situation that is bothering you.

f. Find a hobby that you love and/or start new activities.

This will give your mind something new to focus on so that it does not focus on the things that are bothering you. This will help you feel better and rejuvenate you for when the next work day rolls around.

Expressing your emotions safely and healthily can be a difficult thing for many people, but there are ways to do it that allow you to express yourself effectively without putting yourself or others at risk.

CHAPTER 9: REGULAR SELF-CARE CHECKS

Your mental health and emotional well-being are of the utmost importance to you and those around you, so if something is bothering you or causing problems for you, it is important to address it. Regularly checking your mental health will help you notice any problems as soon as possible so that you can take timely action without making the situation worse.

Better physical and mental health means more fulfilling relationships and better job performance, which leads to more money and benefits. Regularly checking your mental health helps ensure that everything is running smoothly for you, making it easier for you to take action when something does not feel right.

When negative thoughts, feelings, or emotions arise, it isn't easy to know when they are likely to pass. It is common for negative feelings and thoughts to stay with you for some time after the event that caused them, so knowing about them early will help you deal with them. This can help you avoid many problems in future.

Things You Can Do to Check Your Mental State Regularly

1. Use your smartphone or a simple notebook to keep track of your mental health status

Nowadays, the majority of people carry their smartphones with them. These can be used to take notes similar to what you might write in a notebook. Using an app like Evernote is practical because you can type information directly into the program using your smartphone or tablet, back it up to the cloud, and then access it from anywhere with an internet connection.

A record like this can help you remember things that happened, which will help you know why your mental health was affected. This can be helpful for future quick references and determining whether or not something needs to be remembered.

2. Perform a Daily Checkup of Your Mental Health

Use the following checklist to see how you are doing each day mentally. This will help you become more aware of your mental state and keep a record that you can return to in the future. Doing this can help you assess your mental state more clearly, making it easier for you to take action before any problems develop.

Doing this regularly can allow you to make any necessary changes or improvements to your life so that you feel better both mentally and physically.

3. Plan Your Own Quiet Time Every Day.

Having your own quiet time can help in checking your mental state. Most people do not realize that solitude is important to mental health. Solitude will help you clear your mind of all positive and negative thoughts.

- Make sure you have at least 30 minutes of peaceful quiet time every day where you will not be interrupted. If you cannot find the time during your regular waking hours, make sure you reserve that time for yourself before going to bed so you can relax as much as possible before going to sleep.

- Use this as an opportunity to take your mind off whatever you are worrying about or feeling anxious about.

- Use this time as a treat, and be sure not to sacrifice it.

- During this time, it is a good idea to keep a notebook with you and some pens or pencils so you can write down things you need to remember or be creative in other ways. You might want to stick to writing down things in your notebook, as it can be more personal and private.

- Remember that this is not meant to be a punishment, so do not make yourself uncomfortable during the time you have set aside. However, if you feel like the quiet time is not helping, try making it shorter or doing something different during your quiet time.

Having time that you set aside to spend alone every day can help bring order to your daily activities. It will not be hard to do. Just make sure you are using this quiet time for yourself so that it does not become a chore and instead helps you relax and take care of yourself.

Understanding yourself and your mental health can help you put things in perspective and comprehend what is happening when things do not go as planned. This can make it simpler for you to take action on a problem before it gets out of hand.

CONCLUSION

Negative emotions are a part of our everyday experience. They can help clarify problems and motivate us to take action. Like other human capacities, they can be used wisely or unwisely. If we understand their function and learn skills to manage them, negative emotions help us thrive. If we avoid them or try to control or suppress them, our connections to the people and activities that make life worth living will erode.

Thoughts and emotions can have a powerful impact on our physical health. Negative emotions can trigger physical problems such as headaches and backaches, while the presence of negative emotions in your body can affect your overall well-being. Studies show that negative emotions significantly affect your physical health and can even contribute to a host of conditions, including anxiety, depression, heart disease, and cancer. Negative emotions are often expressed in damaging ways, such as engaging in self-destructive behaviors, which can have harmful physical consequences.

Negative emotions tend to motivate people toward destructive behavior that damages the lives of themselves and others, often causing misery for those around them. Resentment, for example, is one of the most destructive feelings. Other feelings that are destructive or harmful when expressed out of control include anger, jealousy, doubt, and hopelessness.

Knowing how to recognize, define, and respond to negative emotions gives us more choice in managing our lives. When we know how to identify what we're feeling and why, our capacity for being effective in the world increases. Managing negative emotions means having more choices about how we respond to stress, disappointment, and frustration. In other words, knowing how to handle negative emotions gives us a wider range of possibilities in our lives, giving us more options for handling the challenges we all face from time to time.

When we learn to distinguish between negative emotions and the thoughts that trigger them, we can begin to work with our emotions rather than being driven by them. Our negative thoughts about our circumstances become more clearly distinguishable from the situations themselves. As a result, we have more personal power over how we respond. We have choices about how we define our situation and what strategies are effective for changing it. This allows us to focus on changing things that can be changed and accepting those that can't. It also allows us to develop more effective strategies for dealing with negative emotions and coping with challenging situations.

Being able to recognize and accept our negative emotions is something we can all improve upon. The skills of understanding how our emotions work, separating them from what they are triggered by, and knowing how to regulate them give us a greater capacity for managing our lives effectively. Understanding our emotions better allows us to make more rational decisions about what we want and need in our lives. And developing effective coping strategies enhances the quality of our lives by enabling us to avoid situations that cause negative emotions.

However, negative emotions are not always so powerful. They can be given space to exist and embraced instead of avoiding or judging them. Positive changes in your life and the lives of those around you can be made by acting on negative emotions in a healthy way. Since every individual is unique and expresses emotions in different ways, there is no one right way to express emotions. Learning how to express your emotions in a way that make the most sense to you is one of the keys to enhancing the quality of your life.

You might find some things easier than others—some will come easily while others take a lot of practice. You'll probably find that you can't do everything all at once, just as you can't have a perfect marriage, children, and a career all at the same time.

That's okay. You'll find balance and will know when to apply which skills. When you decide to use what you learn, whether managing your own emotions or knowing how to identify other people's emotions, the real power comes from practicing what you read about in this book and using it to help you make sense of your feelings and behavior.

This book aims to increase your emotional awareness and teach you how to handle your feelings in a healthy way. It won't tell you what to think or do, but it will demonstrate better ways to comprehend others, yourself, and your surroundings. Then you can use that knowledge as a way of developing personal growth and increasing your effectiveness in the world.

In the end, negative emotions are a part of who you are and can be used for good or bad. When you learn to identify, understand, and healthily express them, negative emotions become manageable and can fuel your well-being.

Changing your behavior can be difficult, and it takes time, but it's possible if you keep at it. Learning new skills takes practice, like any other skill, so the first step is simply understanding that it's okay to make mistakes and keep learning. The emotions that cause you to act in harmful or destructive ways can either be accepted for what they are and changed or allowed to exist in the way they do naturally. You can control your emotions if you actively participate in the change process and make small, daily adjustments as you become more aware of yourself, your life, and your emotions.